The Thyroid Diet Cookbook

Over 70 Healing Recipes to Reverse Hypothyroidism and Hashimoto's Naturally

Lily Bennett

First published by VivaVitality Editions 2024
Copyright © 2024 by Lily Bennett
All rights reserved. No part of this publication may be reproduced, stored or transmitted in any form or by any means, electronic, mechanical, photocopying, recording, scanning, or otherwise without written permission from the publisher. It is illegal to copy this book, post it to a website, or distribute it by any other means without permission.
First edition

Table of Contents

Introduction
Why Diet Matters for Thyroid Health

Chapter 1: Understanding the Thyroid
Thyroid Function Overview
Common Thyroid Disorders: Hypothyroidism & Hashimoto's

Chapter 2: The Role of Diet in Thyroid Health
Iodine: The Essential Building Block
Selenium: The Unsung Hero of Thyroid Health
Zinc: The Regulator of Thyroid Hormones
Iron: The Oxygen Carrier for Thyroid Health
The Subtle Impact of Vitamin D Deficiency
The Role of Fats in Thyroid Hormone Production
The Gut-Thyroid Connection
Blood Sugar and the Thyroid

Chapter 3: Healing Foods Explained
Best Foods for Healing Thyroid Disorders

Chapter 4: Foods to Avoid
Goitrogens and Their Effects
Inflammatory Foods and Thyroid Dysfunction

Chapter 5: Breakfast Recipes
1. Avocado & Spinach Smoothie
2. Berry Coconut Yogurt Bowl
3. Delicious Breakfast Omelette
4. Chia Seed Pudding with Sliced Almonds
5. Protein-Packed Green Smoothie
6. Oatmeal with Walnuts & Blueberries
7. Ground Grass-fed Beef with Bell Peppers and Onions
8. Coconut Flour Pancakes
9. Egg & Avocado Toast on Gluten-Free Bread
10. Quinoa Breakfast Bowl with Almonds & Berries
11. Smoked Salmon, Scramble Eggs & Avocado
12. Chia & Almond Butter Smoothie

13. Coconut Yogurt Bowl with Nuts and Berries
14. Quinoa Porridge with Apple, Banana and Berries
15. Breakfast Bowl with Poached Egg, Quinoa, Avocado, Cherry Tomatoes, and Pesto

Chapter 6: Lunch Recipes
1. Grilled Chicken Bowl with White Rice and Avocado
2. Shrimp and Basmati Rice Bowl with Steamed Vegetables
3. Grilled Turkey with Quinoa, Broccoli, and Bell Peppers
4. Salmon Sushi Rice Bowl with Cucumber and Avocado
5. Lentil and Spinach Soup with Fresh Herbs
6. Mediterranean Sardine Salad
7. Chicken and Basmati Rice Bowl with cucumbers, tomatoes and olives
8. Turkey Curry with Basmati Rice
9. Savory Sunday Lunch with Shredded Beef, Rice, and Fried Plantains
10. Grilled Salmon with Asparagus and Roasted Sweet Potatoes
11. Grilled Shrimp Salad with Cherry Tomatoes and Bell Peppers
12. Fresh Tuna Salad with Avocado, Cherry Tomatoes
13. Quinoa Chickpea Salad Bowl with Cucumber and Tomatoes
14. Beef Pho (Vietnamese Noodle Soup)
15. Fish Stew with Vegetables
16. Grilled Honey Garlic Salmon with Brown Rice
17. Chicken Fried Rice with Vegetables and a Fried Egg
18. Mediterranean Grilled Chicken Salad
19. Garlic Shrimp with Zucchini Noodles, Cherry Tomatoes, and Olives
20. Thyroid-Friendly Bibimbap (Korean Rice Bowl)

Chapter 7: Dinner Recipes
1. Grilled Chicken with Quinoa and Roasted Vegetables
2. Grilled Salmon with Butternut Squash Purée
3. Grilled Lamb Chops with Rosemary Sweet Potato Fries
4. Grilled Filet Mignon with Garlic Mashed Potatoes
5. Stuffed Bell Peppers
6. Grilled Steak with Rosemary, Asparagus, and Roasted Potatoe
7. Grilled Salmon with Quinoa and Roasted Vegetables
8. Hearty Beef Stew with Root Vegetables
9. Grilled Chicken Fajitas with Bell Peppers and Onions
10. Japanese Grilled Mackerel with Rice and Vegetables
11. Savory Shrimp Soup
12. Chicken and Vegetable Stir-Fry

13. Creamy Mushroom Risotto
14. Shredded Beef Tacos
15. Lamb Kebab and Vegetable Skewers
16. Lemon Garlic Baked Cod
17. Gourmet Steak Dinner with Mashed Sweet Potatoes and Sautéed Kale
18. Braised Chicken with Pearl Onions and Mushrooms
19. Crispy Crusted Fish
20. Herb-Roasted Whole Chicken with Crispy Potatoes
21. Herb-Crusted Rack of Lamb with Mashed Potatoes
22. Beef Fajitas with Guacamole
23. Grilled Steak with Roasted Sweet Potatoes and Fresh Arugula Salad
24. Roasted Duck with Rosemary, Potatoes, and Carrots
25. Shrimp Paella

Chapter 8: Snacks and Appetizers
1. Almond Butter and Apple Slices
2. Sliced Avocado with Lemon and Sea Salt
3. Boiled Eggs with Olive Oil Drizzle
4. Brazil Nuts and Blueberries
5. Avocado and Cherry Tomato Cup
6. Thyroid-Boosting Smoothie
7. Coconut Yogurt with Walnuts and Honey
8. Carrot Sticks with Red Pepper Hummus
9. Celery Sticks with Almond Butter
10. Thyroid-Friendly Energy Bites

Chapter 9: Desserts
1. Almond Flour Chocolate Chip Cookies
2. Dairy-Free Coconut Ice Cream
3. Gluten-Free Apple Crisp Recipe
4. Chocolate Avocado Mousse
5. Coconut Macaroons
6. Baked Pears with Cinnamon and Walnuts
7. Cashew Date Energy Balls
8. Banana Almond Nice Cream
9. Frozen Coconut Yogurt Bark with Berries and Almonds
10. No-Bake Chocolate Coconut Bars

Conclusion

Introduction: Why Diet Matters for Thyroid Health

Your thyroid is a tiny, butterfly-shaped gland nestled at the base of your neck, yet it wields a surprisingly big impact on your whole body! It's super important for keeping your metabolism in check, managing how your body uses energy, generates heat, and supports essential functions like heart rate, digestion, and even your mood! When the thyroid is working well, it often goes unnoticed, but when it gets out of whack—like with hypothyroidism or Hashimoto's disease—the effects can be felt in every part of the body.

Lately, there's been a lot of buzz about how our diet can impact thyroid health! Today, we understand that food can be an amazing ally for thyroid health, helping to ease symptoms and even repair some of the effects of autoimmune thyroid issues, unlike what we knew a decade ago. However, food isn't a magical solution for everything. It's a journey that blends understanding, a sprinkle of patience, and a dash of consistency! Let's kick off our adventure: discovering how making the right food choices can support, nurture, and safeguard your thyroid, empowering you to enjoy a vibrant and energetic life!

The Silent Power of Nutrients

Many of us are raised thinking that food is just for filling our bellies, but the true magic of food is in its incredible ability to energize and nurture our bodies. This is particularly the case with the thyroid! Nutrients like iodine, selenium, zinc, and vitamin D play a vital role in keeping our thyroid gland healthy and happy! Many of us find ourselves in a world where our diets are packed with processed foods, yet we're missing out on those essential nutrients! The typical Western diet is packed with sugars, refined grains, and unhealthy fats—ingredients that aren't doing any favors for the thyroid. On the flip side, they can stir up inflammation and throw hormones out of whack, which might make thyroid issues even trickier to manage.

Guess what? There's some great news! With some smart tweaks to your diet, you can transform the nutritional vibe in your body, setting the stage for happy thyroid health! The foods you choose can be your thyroid's best friends or its worst foes! This cookbook is all about showing you the wonderful healing foods that can team up with your body to help reduce inflammation, boost your immune system, and give your thyroid the nutrients it craves for peak performance.

Selenium, found in delicious foods like Brazil nuts, sunflower seeds, and some fish, is super important for how our thyroid hormones work! Interestingly, research indicates that a lack of selenium is frequently associated with autoimmune thyroid conditions such as Hashimoto's. Iodine is a vital ingredient for thyroid hormones, and it's important to have just the right amount! Finding the perfect balance is key for thyroid function, and exploring natural food sources can make it a fun journey!

Finding that perfect mix of nutrients—ensuring you have just the right amount without going overboard—is key to keeping your thyroid happy and healthy! While supplements can be helpful, nothing beats whole foods as your top source of these nutrients! A thoughtfully crafted diet goes beyond just being a substitute for medication or supplements. This is your exciting first step towards taking charge of your body!

Inflammation and the Thyroid: A Vicious Cycle

The connection between thyroid health and inflammation is often overlooked! Chronic inflammation is on the rise in today's world, and it plays a significant role in autoimmune conditions such as Hashimoto's. The foods we choose can either spark inflammation or help calm it down, and when it comes to your thyroid, this difference is super important!

Some foods, such as processed grains, sugars, and unhealthy fats, can get the immune system a bit too excited, causing it to mistakenly go after healthy cells and create a bit of chaos. This poses a unique risk for the thyroid, as autoimmune thyroid conditions arise when the body inadvertently targets the thyroid gland itself. As time goes on, this ongoing attack can make the thyroid less effective, resulting in hormone imbalances that can influence energy levels, metabolism, and mood.

On the bright side, anti-inflammatory foods packed with antioxidants and omega-3 fatty acids can be a delightful way to calm the immune system, easing inflammation and helping to manage the autoimmune response. Many people with thyroid disorders notice a wonderful boost in their symptoms when they switch to an anti-inflammatory diet. Wild-caught salmon, leafy greens, turmeric, and blueberries are not just tasty treats; they also work wonders in reducing inflammation and safeguarding the thyroid from additional harm.

It's not only about cutting out the bad stuff—it's also about adding in the goodies that help reduce inflammation and support thyroid health! By incorporating more anti-inflammatory foods into your diet, you're creating a friendly environment for your thyroid, helping it thrive and tackle the challenges of autoimmune conditions with a little extra support!

Your Gut: The Key to Thyroid Health

We can't chat about thyroid health without giving a nod to the gut! Many experts now think that gut health plays a super important role in managing thyroid conditions! Did you know? Around 70% of your immune system is hanging out in your gut! If your gut health isn't quite right—whether it's due to leaky gut, an imbalance of gut bacteria, or ongoing digestive troubles—your immune system might just be a bit too active and not in perfect harmony.

An energetic immune system plays a significant role in autoimmune thyroid conditions such as Hashimoto's. When your gut barrier isn't at its best, bits of undigested food, toxins, and pesky bacteria can sneak into your bloodstream, setting off an immune reaction. As time goes on, this persistent immune response can begin to focus on not only the gut but also other areas of the body, like the thyroid.

So, what's in it for you? The foods you enjoy can have an influence on your gut health, which in turn affects your thyroid! Transforming your gut health with the right foods can significantly ease the symptoms of thyroid issues, like tiredness, weight fluctuations, and that pesky brain fog. Begin by adding some delicious foods packed with probiotics to your meals, such as tangy fermented veggies like sauerkraut and kimchi, along with creamy yogurt, to bring some friendly bacteria into your gut! Meanwhile, fiber-packed foods such as chia seeds, flaxseeds, and leafy greens serve as a delightful feast for the good bacteria, helping to nurture a happy and balanced microbiome!

Nourishing your gut does wonders! It boosts digestion and immune function while also setting up a cozy environment for your thyroid to thrive. Healing begins inside us, and often, the gut is the perfect place to kick off that adventure.

Tailoring Your Thyroid Diet Just for You

It's essential to recognize that when it comes to managing thyroid health through diet, there's no universal solution that works for everyone. What works for one person might not be the best fit for someone else, so it's important to listen to your body's individual needs. Making things personal is essential!

Some folks with thyroid concerns may find themselves a bit sensitive to certain goitrogens—those interesting compounds in cruciferous veggies like broccoli, cauliflower, and kale, which can play a role in thyroid hormone production when consumed in larger quantities. For some, these veggies might not make much of a difference and can be enjoyed on a regular basis! Discovering how to tune in to your body and tweak your diet can be a journey!

This book is packed with delightful recipes that steer clear of common thyroid disruptors like gluten and soy, and they're super easy to customize to fit your unique preferences! If you find that some foods seem to amplify your symptoms, consider that a helpful hint from your body! A thyroid-friendly diet is all about embracing flexibility and discovering the delicious foods that make you feel your best!

As you tweak your diet over time, you'll begin to see changes not only in your thyroid health but also in how great you feel overall! Your energy will soar, mental clarity will shine through, and that extra weight that felt like a challenge might just start to fade away! Discover the magic of a personalized diet—it's all about tuning into your body's signals and honoring what it truly needs!

The Magic of Consistency

The key takeaway for diet and thyroid health is all about the magic of consistency! One healthy meal might not transform your thyroid in an instant, but consistently enjoying nourishing, thyroid-friendly meals can make a wonderful difference over time! It's all about incorporating little, sustainable tweaks that seamlessly fit into your everyday life!

This book is filled with recipes that make it easy and fun to bring healing foods into your everyday life! From a refreshing smoothie to kickstart your morning to a cozy dinner that wraps up your day, every recipe is a stepping stone toward enhancing your thyroid health. Keep in mind, each bite matters!

As you set off on this adventure, remember to be kind to yourself! Healing is a journey, and diet is just one fun part of the adventure! It's a vital aspect—something you can influence each and every day! Every time you make a nourishing choice, you're giving your thyroid the boost it craves to work its magic, helping you feel fantastic!

Chapter 1: Understanding the Thyroid

Thyroid Function Overview

The thyroid may be tiny, but it plays a big role in keeping our bodies running smoothly! It serves as the heart of your body's metabolism, energy management, and hormonal harmony. The thyroid works its magic quietly, handling its responsibilities effortlessly and without drawing too much attention. However, when it stumbles, the impact can be quite extensive, often leading us to deal with tiredness, changes in weight, and a bit of emotional rollercoaster.

Getting to know the thyroid's function starts with appreciating how it helps keep our metabolism in check. The thyroid is a gland that creates hormones—namely triiodothyronine (T3) and thyroxine (T4)—that zip through the bloodstream, impacting almost every cell in our bodies! These hormones play a critical role in how quickly our bodies turn food into energy, keep our hearts beating just right, and help maintain our body temperature. This process is commonly known as the "metabolic rate," and it helps keep the body balanced. Imagine it as the body's little thermostat; the thyroid fine-tunes everything based on what it thinks is necessary.

The brain takes the lead in controlling the thyroid, with the hypothalamus and pituitary gland playing key roles in this fascinating process. The hypothalamus keeps an eye on what the body needs and, when it notices a drop in energy or metabolism, it sends a little nudge to the pituitary gland. The pituitary gland jumps into action by releasing thyroid-stimulating hormone (TSH), which tells the thyroid to kick it up a notch and produce more T3 and T4. It's a wonderfully crafted feedback loop, made to keep the body's energy use just right! However, when things take a turn—be it due to a nutritional gap, stress, or an autoimmune reaction—this system can get a bit wobbly, resulting in either too little or too much thyroid hormone production.

Although it might be easy to view the thyroid as just the body's metabolic engine, its responsibilities go well beyond merely burning calories. It helps in a variety of processes, affecting everything from heart rate to brain function to skin health. When thyroid hormone levels are right, they keep our hearts beating, support the renewal of our cells and tissues, and boost our brainpower, helping with focus, memory, and a stable mood.

So, what occurs when the thyroid starts to struggle a bit? Let's dive into how even the tiniest shifts in thyroid function can show up throughout the body!

When thyroid hormone levels dip too low—a condition called hypothyroidism—the metabolism takes a little break. Imagine attempting to run a marathon at a leisurely pace: everything seems to move at a relaxed tempo, from your physical energy to your mental clarity. This sluggishness not only leaves you feeling drained, but also affects your digestion, immune system, and emotional well-being. Individuals with underactive thyroids may find themselves facing unexpected weight gain, even when their diet and exercise routines remain unchanged. In addition to physical symptoms, low thyroid levels can create a bit of a mental haze, making it tricky to think clearly or recall even the simplest things.

On the flip side, we have hyperthyroidism, a condition where the thyroid goes into overdrive and produces an excess of hormones. In this scenario, the metabolism kicks into high gear, which can lead to weight loss, a bit of irritability, and a burst of nervous energy! Individuals with hyperthyroidism may experience a whirlwind of sensations, including racing thoughts, a quickened heartbeat, and some difficulty catching those Z's. The body is really revving up, using energy reserves at a pace that's hard to keep up with!

Here's a fun fact that might surprise you: both underactive and overactive thyroid conditions often stem from the same root issue—a hiccup in the feedback loop that keeps thyroid hormone production in check. This breakdown can happen due to various reasons, including autoimmune diseases such as Hashimoto's and Graves' disease, as well as nutritional imbalances and ongoing stress. Getting to the heart of the matter is essential for tackling thyroid issues in a smart way!

The thyroid's main role is hormone production, but its well-being is shaped by a variety of factors, such as lifestyle choices, nutrient intake, and stress levels. The thyroid is quite responsive to shifts in the body's internal environment. For example, some nutrients such as iodine and selenium play a vital role in the production of thyroid hormones. When there isn't enough iodine, the thyroid struggles to make enough T3 and T4, which can result in hypothyroidism. Selenium plays a fun role in transforming the less active T4 into the more powerful T3, making sure the body gets all the thyroid hormones it needs to keep things running smoothly!

It's not only about fueling your body with the right nutrients—it's also about managing stress along the way! The thyroid has a fascinating link to how our body handles stress! When we're dealing with chronic stress, our adrenal glands kick into gear and release cortisol. This hormone can be quite beneficial in short bursts, but if it sticks around for too long, it can cause some trouble for the thyroid. Cortisol can slow down the transformation of T4 into T3, the active thyroid hormone, which can lead to a bit of an imbalance in the body. Chronic stress can lead to a slowdown in hormone production by the thyroid, which might result in symptoms of hypothyroidism, even when the thyroid gland is perfectly healthy!

Keeping your thyroid in tip-top shape requires a balanced approach! Focusing on just one nutrient or trying to ramp up thyroid hormone production isn't the whole story; it's important to see the bigger picture! Your thyroid is part of a system that connects your brain, stress levels, diet, and even your immune function! Embracing a well-rounded approach to thyroid health—focusing on your nutrition, keeping stress in check, and nurturing your body's feedback loops—can help this small but powerful gland thrive at its peak performance.

Common Thyroid Disorders: Hypothyroidism & Hashimoto's

Thyroid disorders have a sneaky way of making their presence known—often gradually and quietly—until they change how we feel about our overall well-being. Hypothyroidism and Hashimoto's thyroiditis are two of the most common thyroid conditions, and although they might seem like different problems, they're actually closely connected. Grasping both conditions opens up a view into the connection between our immune system and thyroid function, and it gives us the tools to tackle and manage those symptoms that can throw us off balance.

Hypothyroidism: When the Thyroid Slows Down

Hypothyroidism, commonly known as an "underactive thyroid," happens when the thyroid gland doesn't produce enough thyroid hormones—namely T3 and T4. These hormones play a vital role in managing metabolism, which is all about how our body transforms food into energy! When the thyroid takes it easy, everything else in the body tends to slow down too! While it may seem straightforward—less hormone means a slower metabolism—the effects can be wide-ranging and, at times, quite challenging.

The signs of hypothyroidism can be a bit tricky to spot initially, showing up as a touch of fatigue, some stubborn extra pounds, or that hazy feeling in your head. However, if not addressed, the condition can gradually get worse, resulting in challenges like overwhelming fatigue, feelings of sadness, and a dip in motivation. Many folks start to see some changes in their skin, hair, and nails—think dry, flaky skin, thinning hair, and brittle nails, which are all typical signs of an underactive thyroid.

The thyroid plays a key role in regulating body temperature, so people with hypothyroidism might feel a bit chilly, even when everyone else is cozy and warm! At first glance, this might seem like a quirky little detail, but when you combine it with other signs—such as joint pain, a slower heart rate, and constipation—the intriguing picture of hypothyroidism starts to unfold! The body's systems, especially metabolism, are moving at a leisurely pace, and the thyroid is the star of the show!

Diagnosing hypothyroidism can be a bit tricky at times. It's interesting to note that many symptoms can be similar to those of other conditions, and quite a few people might go for years with hypothyroidism without even knowing what's causing their discomfort! A key sign of hypothyroidism is higher levels of TSH. When the thyroid isn't cranking out enough T3 and T4, the pituitary gland kicks into gear and produces more TSH to give the thyroid a little nudge to get going. Elevated TSH levels in blood tests can be a hint that your thyroid might need some attention!

Managing hypothyroidism is about more than simply adjusting hormone levels. It's all about helping the body get back to its normal groove, often by mixing in some lifestyle tweaks, a balanced diet, and sometimes a little medication! Although synthetic thyroid hormones can be beneficial in restoring balance, tackling the root causes—like nutrient deficiencies or chronic inflammation—can truly transform how one feels in the long run.

Hashimoto's Thyroiditis: The Autoimmune Attack

So, let's talk about where Hashimoto's comes into play! Hypothyroidism is a general term that describes an underactive thyroid, and one of the most common culprits behind it is Hashimoto's thyroiditis, especially in the United States. Hashimoto's stands out because it's an autoimmune disease! This means the immune system gets a bit confused and thinks the thyroid gland is a foe, leading it to launch an attack.

Autoimmune diseases such as Hashimoto's involve more than just the thyroid being targeted; they also stem from an immune system that's a bit too eager, leading to some unintended consequences. It's a bit of a mystery, but sometimes the immune system gets confused and starts making antibodies that mistakenly go after the thyroid gland. As time goes on, this attack affects the thyroid tissue, making it harder for it to produce hormones.

Individuals with Hashimoto's frequently encounter similar symptoms to those with hypothyroidism, such as fatigue, weight gain, brain fog, and feelings of depression. Since this condition is linked to the immune system, symptoms can vary and may occasionally resemble those of other autoimmune conditions. Sometimes, Hashimoto's can lead to a brief episode of hyperthyroidism as the immune system has a little tussle with the gland, sending extra thyroid hormones into the bloodstream. This might cause some moments of anxiety, a quickened heartbeat, and unexpected weight loss. As time goes on, the thyroid may get more and more damaged, leading to a lasting case of hypothyroidism.

Diagnosing Hashimoto's means looking at more than just TSH levels; it also includes checking for specific thyroid antibodies like anti-thyroid peroxidase (TPO) antibodies and anti-thyroglobulin antibodies. High levels of these antibodies in the blood are clear signs that the immune system is on a mission to target the thyroid!

But this is where hope comes into play! Although Hashimoto's may not be "cured" in the usual way—once an autoimmune condition starts, it can't just be turned back—it can definitely be managed. One of the most exciting parts of managing Hashimoto's is tackling the root causes of autoimmune activity, especially chronic inflammation and gut health! Lots of people discover that by embracing an anti-inflammatory diet, managing stress, and tackling nutrient gaps (like iodine, selenium, and zinc), they can really cut down on how often and how intensely flare-ups occur.

It's essential to keep in mind that even though Hashimoto's is an autoimmune disease, the thyroid can frequently regain a lot of its function if we can slow down or stop the immune attack. It's super important for those with Hashimoto's to embrace a lifestyle that promotes immune harmony and reduces the triggers that can spark autoimmune activity.

The Relationship Between Hypothyroidism and Hashimoto's

It's clear how hypothyroidism and Hashimoto's are linked! Hashimoto's is a major player in the world of hypothyroidism, particularly in developed countries. Not everyone with hypothyroidism has Hashimoto's, but many who do may find themselves facing an underactive thyroid due to the immune system's ongoing antics. The main distinction lies in the root cause: hypothyroidism can stem from things like nutrient deficiencies or thyroid surgery, whereas Hashimoto's is fueled by the immune system itself.

Both conditions, however, have a shared aim in treatment—bringing back harmony. No matter if it's an autoimmune disorder or a sluggish thyroid at play, the aim remains consistent: alleviate symptoms, balance thyroid hormone levels, and enhance overall wellness through diet, lifestyle choices, and occasionally medical help.

Chapter 2: The Role of Diet in Thyroid Health

The saying "you are what you eat" really shines when we talk about thyroid health. Your diet is more than just fuel for daily activities; it's also the foundation for essential hormones and helps keep your body in perfect harmony.

Getting to know how diet influences the thyroid starts with recognizing its special connection with nutrients. The thyroid needs certain vitamins, minerals, and macronutrients to create hormones, react to brain signals, and bounce back when it's feeling stressed. If these nutrients aren't at the right levels, the thyroid might not work as smoothly, leading to some ups and downs, or it could even take a break entirely!

Iodine: The Essential Building Block

Iodine is probably the most famous nutrient linked to thyroid health! This trace mineral plays a crucial role in the production of thyroid hormones, particularly T3 (triiodothyronine) and T4 (thyroxine). The names of these hormones come from the number of iodine molecules they have, and without enough iodine, the thyroid can't produce the hormones needed to keep the body's metabolism in check. In parts of the world where iodine is lacking, goiters (enlarged thyroid glands) pop up frequently, serving as a noticeable indicator that the thyroid is hustling to keep up with the body's demands. Goiters are becoming rarer in places where iodine is added to table salt and various foods, but iodine deficiency still pops up and plays a big role in hypothyroidism.

What's really interesting, though, is that iodine isn't just about how much you have—it's also about finding the right balance! Not enough iodine can lead to hypothyroidism, but having too much can also spark thyroid issues. Dietary sources of iodine, like seaweed, fish, and dairy products, are super important! These foods offer iodine in just the right amounts for the body to use effectively! When it comes to supplementation, it's important to tread carefully! Too much iodine can rev up the thyroid a bit too much or even make autoimmune conditions like Hashimoto's thyroiditis a little trickier to manage.

Selenium: The Unsung Hero of Thyroid Health

While iodine often steals the spotlight, selenium is another important player in thyroid health that tends to be overlooked. Selenium is a fantastic antioxidant that plays a key role in shielding the thyroid from oxidative stress, which happens when free radicals outnumber the body's natural defenses. The thyroid is especially prone to oxidative stress because it produces hormones at a high rate. Each time the thyroid cranks out T4, it also lets loose some hydrogen peroxide as a little extra. While it's a natural byproduct, too much of it can be a bit troublesome! Selenium works its magic by neutralizing those pesky free radicals, keeping the thyroid safe from inflammation and harm!

Additionally, selenium plays a key role in transforming T4 into T3, which is the more active and powerful thyroid hormone. If there's not enough selenium, the body might have plenty of T4 but could still face hypothyroid symptoms since T4 isn't being converted into T3 effectively. Brazil nuts, sardines, and sunflower seeds are fantastic natural sources of selenium! Adding them to your diet can really give your thyroid function a nice little boost.

Zinc: The Regulator of Thyroid Hormones

Zinc is another key nutrient for keeping your thyroid happy! This essential mineral plays a vital role in making thyroid hormones and helping to keep your immune system in check. Zinc teams up with selenium to help convert T4 into the active T3, and it also helps keep the thyroid-stimulating hormone (TSH) stable, which is made by the pituitary gland to manage thyroid function.

Zinc deficiency is more prevalent than most people think, especially among those who embrace vegetarian or vegan diets, since plant-based foods usually offer lower amounts of bioavailable zinc than their animal-based counterparts. Lack of enough zinc can really impact how well your body makes and manages thyroid hormones, which might result in some hypothyroid symptoms popping up.

For a natural zinc boost, try adding delicious foods like oysters, beef, pumpkin seeds, and chickpeas to your meals! These tasty foods offer a great source of zinc that can boost both thyroid and immune function, especially for those who might be at risk of not getting enough.

Iron: The Oxygen Carrier for Thyroid Health

Iron plays a significant role in how well the thyroid functions. Iron is super important for making thyroid peroxidase, an enzyme that's crucial for producing those vital thyroid hormones! When there's not enough iron, the thyroid struggles to produce T3 and T4 effectively, which can result in hypothyroidism. Plus, iron helps carry oxygen all around the body, and not having enough can lead to feelings of tiredness, weakness, and other signs often linked to anemia and hypothyroidism.

Iron deficiency often pops up in women of childbearing age, thanks to menstruation, and it can get a little worse with diets that skimp on iron-rich goodies like red meat, leafy greens, and legumes. For those embracing vegetarian or vegan lifestyles, keeping an eye on iron intake is key! Plant-based iron, known as non-heme iron, isn't absorbed by the body as easily as the heme iron found in animal products.

Try pairing iron-rich foods with vibrant vitamin C-packed options like citrus fruits or bell peppers. This delightful combo not only enhances bioavailability but also supports your thyroid function.

The Subtle Impact of Vitamin D Deficiency

Vitamin D may not be the star player in making thyroid hormones, but it certainly shines when it comes to supporting the immune system and keeping inflammation in check—two important aspects for anyone dealing with autoimmune thyroid issues like Hashimoto's. Research indicates that people with thyroid disorders frequently experience low vitamin D levels, which could make their situation a bit trickier by affecting their immune system.

Getting enough vitamin D from food can be a bit tricky, especially if you live in places where the sun doesn't shine much. So, a supplementation can be the perfect solution to keep those levels up! Keeping your vitamin D levels right can boost your immune system and may help lower the chances of thyroid inflammation or autoimmune flare-ups.

The Role of Fats in Thyroid Hormone Production

Fats sometimes get a bit of a bad rap in health talks, but when it comes to thyroid function, they're actually super important! The thyroid gland really pays attention to shifts in fat intake, especially regarding the balance of omega-3 and omega-6 fatty acids. Omega-3s, which you can find in delicious fatty fish like salmon, mackerel, and sardines, as well as in flaxseeds and walnuts, are fantastic for reducing inflammation and keeping your thyroid gland happy and healthy! Omega-6s, however, can be a bit of a troublemaker! When we eat too many of them—something that's pretty typical in the standard Western diet—they can stir up chronic inflammation, which isn't great for our thyroid function.

Finding the right balance of these fats is essential for keeping inflammation in check and giving a boost to the thyroid's hormone production! This involves actively choosing to add more omega-3-rich foods to your diet while cutting back on those processed oils high in omega-6, like those in fried and packaged goodies. Both types of fat play important roles in our health, but it's really all about how we balance them in our diets!

The Gut-Thyroid Connection

One of the most intriguing discoveries in recent years is the strong link between gut health and thyroid function. The gut is more than just a digestion hub—it's like a lively command center for immune function and hormone production! Research indicates that the well-being of the gut microbiome, which consists of trillions of bacteria residing in the digestive tract, can have a direct impact on the efficiency of thyroid function. When your gut is feeling a bit off or inflamed, a situation called dysbiosis, it can throw a wrench in the conversion of T4 to T3 and raise the chances of autoimmune issues like Hashimoto's thyroiditis.

A diet that's packed with processed foods, sugars, and unhealthy fats can really shake up the gut's microbiome, making it harder for the body to soak up nutrients and potentially causing some inflammation along the way. On the bright side, a diet filled with whole, unprocessed foods nurtures a lively and healthy microbiome, enhancing nutrient absorption and encouraging a balanced immune response. Adding delicious probiotic foods such as yogurt, kefir, sauerkraut, and kimchi, along with prebiotic fibers from garlic, onions, and bananas, to your meals can be a fun way to support a happy gut, which also plays a role in keeping your thyroid in check.

Blood Sugar and the Thyroid

The link between diet and thyroid health goes beyond just nutrients to include the aspect of blood sugar regulation. The thyroid is quite responsive to changes in blood sugar levels, and ongoing imbalances—whether due to too much sugar or inconsistent eating patterns—can affect how well the thyroid works. When blood sugar levels go up and down often, the body feels stressed, leading to the release of cortisol. This hormone can be quite handy in short bursts, but when it sticks around for too long, it might throw a wrench in thyroid hormone production.

Enjoying balanced meals that mix protein, healthy fats, and fiber can be a delightful way to keep blood sugar levels steady and lower cortisol production. Maintaining this balance is especially crucial for those with thyroid disorders, as keeping blood sugar steady can boost energy, lift mood, and enhance overall thyroid function.

A Diet That Supports the Thyroid

The foods you choose can really influence how well your thyroid works! A diet packed with essential nutrients such as iodine and selenium, balanced with healthy fats, and friendly to gut health lays the groundwork for fantastic thyroid function. By exploring how these dietary factors impact your thyroid, you can take proactive steps to support this essential gland, lowering the chances of dysfunction and enhancing your overall health and happiness.

Chapter 3: Healing Foods Explained

The foods you select can truly impact your body's performance, your overall well-being, and your thyroid's ability to tackle its challenges when it comes to healing thyroid disorders. Your diet is more than just fuel; it's a delightful way to give your body the special nutrients and compounds it craves to heal, rebuild, and flourish! The thyroid is quite responsive to our diet, and picking the right foods can really help calm inflammation, balance hormone levels, and boost overall thyroid health.

Discovering the foods that are great for your thyroid health involves exploring how they work with your body. Certain foods are fantastic for giving your thyroid a boost by packing in vital nutrients such as iodine, selenium, and zinc. Plus, there are options that can help ease the inflammation that often tags along with thyroid issues like hypothyroidism and Hashimoto's thyroiditis. Let's dive into some fantastic foods that can help support healing for those dealing with thyroid disorders!

Seaweed: Nature's Iodine-Rich Superfood

When we consider thyroid health, one of the first nutrients that pops into our minds is iodine, the vital building block of thyroid hormones. When there's not enough iodine, the thyroid has a tough time making the hormones it needs to keep our metabolism, energy levels, and overall health in check. Did you know that while iodine is commonly found in table salt, one of the best natural sources of this essential mineral is none other than seaweed? Varieties like nori, wakame, and kombu are packed with iodine, making them fantastic choices for your diet if you want to give your thyroid function a little lift!

Seaweed is a fantastic source of iodine and brings along a treasure trove of other trace minerals like magnesium and calcium that are great for your overall health! These minerals help keep the body in harmony and can ease the effects of stress on the thyroid. Adding seaweed to your soups, salads, or enjoying it as a snack is a fun and tasty way to support your thyroid health!

It's essential to keep an eye on your iodine intake! Seaweed is packed with benefits, but it's good to keep in mind that too much iodine can get the thyroid a bit too excited, particularly for those with autoimmune thyroid issues. Finding the right balance is essential—savoring seaweed a couple of times a week is just the right amount to enjoy its perks without overwhelming your body.

Brazil Nuts: Your Go-To for Selenium

Selenium plays a vital role in keeping your thyroid happy, and guess what? Brazil nuts are packed with this essential mineral! This mineral does double duty: it shields the thyroid from oxidative stress during hormone production and is crucial for transforming thyroid hormone T4 into its more active version, T3. Lack of selenium can leave the thyroid open to harm, making it tricky for the body to use thyroid hormones properly.

A couple of Brazil nuts—just two to three each day—can cover your whole daily selenium needs! They're a tasty and easy option for boosting thyroid health! In addition to selenium, Brazil nuts are packed with healthy fats and a variety of minerals that support overall well-being, making them an ideal snack for anyone dealing with thyroid disorders.

If Brazil nuts aren't your thing, no worries! You can also find selenium in tasty options like sardines, turkey, and sunflower seeds. Adding these to your diet can help keep your thyroid happy and working smoothly in producing and regulating hormones.

Fatty Fish: Omega-3s to Tackle Inflammation

Fatty fish like salmon, mackerel, and sardines are fantastic sources of omega-3 fatty acids, which play a key role in keeping inflammation at bay in the body. Inflammation plays a significant role in various thyroid disorders, especially in autoimmune conditions such as Hashimoto's thyroiditis. Adding more omega-3-rich foods to your meals can be a delightful way to soothe those inflammatory responses that might be affecting your thyroid.

Omega-3s are fantastic for reducing inflammation and also play a key role in supporting brain health, heart health, and overall cellular function, all of which can be influenced by thyroid disorders. Along with fatty fish, you can also discover plant-based omega-3s in flaxseeds, chia seeds, and walnuts. Just keep in mind that the body doesn't convert plant-based omega-3s as efficiently as those from fish. Mixing both fish and plant-based omega-3 sources can be a fantastic way to tackle thyroid inflammation!

If you're not a fish fan, a top-notch fish oil supplement can be a great option! Just remember, it's always best to grab your nutrients from whole foods when you can.

Leafy Greens: Nutrient-Dense Powerhouses

Dark, leafy greens such as spinach, kale, and swiss chard are packed with vitamins and minerals that are great for your thyroid health, including iron, magnesium, and vitamin A. Iron plays a key role in producing thyroid hormones, as it's essential for the enzyme thyroid peroxidase, which aids in the creation of T3 and T4.

Leafy greens not only offer essential nutrients but are also brimming with antioxidants that work wonders in reducing inflammation and oxidative stress, factors that can lead to thyroid issues over time. Adding a mix of leafy greens to your meals—be it in salads, smoothies, or lightly sautéed with garlic—can offer a delightful boost of nutrients that are great for your thyroid health!

Some people with thyroid disorders might fret over eating cruciferous veggies like kale because of their goitrogen content, but no need to worry! Enjoying these nutrient-packed vegetables in moderation is usually safe and can be quite beneficial. Cooking cruciferous vegetables can help minimize their goitrogenic effects, making them a fantastic choice for a thyroid-friendly diet!

Eggs: A Complete Source of Nutrients

Eggs are a fantastic food packed with nutrients, offering a delightful source of iodine, selenium, and zinc—essential elements for keeping your thyroid happy and healthy! The yolk is packed with a treasure trove of nutrients, so it's definitely worth enjoying the whole egg instead of just the whites!

Besides their thyroid-specific perks, eggs pack a punch as a fantastic source of high-quality protein! This is super important for keeping muscle mass in check, balancing blood sugar, and boosting energy levels—all of which can take a hit for those dealing with thyroid issues. Adding eggs to your meals a few times a week is a simple and delightful way to give your thyroid the nutrients it craves for optimal performance.

Berries: Antioxidant Powerhouses

Finally, berries like blueberries, raspberries, and strawberries are packed with antioxidants that help shield the thyroid from oxidative damage. This is especially crucial for individuals with autoimmune thyroid conditions, as the immune system's assault on the thyroid can result in inflammation and tissue damage. Antioxidants work their magic by neutralizing free radicals, which helps to minimize damage and keep thyroid function in tip-top shape!

Berries are not only low in calories but also packed with fiber, making them a fantastic choice for anyone looking to manage their weight, especially for those navigating the challenges of hypothyroidism. Adding a mix of vibrant berries to your daily meals can boost your overall health and give your thyroid a little extra love by fighting off oxidative stress!

Chapter 4: Foods to Avoid

Goitrogens and Their Effects

Goitrogens are natural compounds found in some foods that might affect how the thyroid works. The term originates from "goiter," which describes the swelling of the thyroid gland. This can happen when the thyroid is working overtime to produce hormones. For those navigating thyroid disorders, especially hypothyroidism, the idea of goitrogens can sometimes feel a bit puzzling and worrisome. Could these compounds be harmful? Should we steer clear of them completely? Could there be a more subtle way to weave goitrogenic foods into a diet that supports thyroid health?

To get a handle on how goitrogens influence the thyroid, it's essential to first understand the basic way these compounds work. Goitrogens mainly impact the thyroid by disrupting the absorption of iodine, which is essential for creating the thyroid hormones T3 and T4. Iodine plays a crucial role in helping the thyroid create hormones, and when goitrogens block iodine absorption, the thyroid has to put in extra effort to keep things running smoothly. As time goes on, this added pressure can cause the thyroid to swell up (goiter) and make hormone production drop even more, making issues like hypothyroidism even trickier to manage.

The Types of Goitrogens

Goitrogens come in all shapes and sizes, and you can find them in a mix of foods, especially in some veggies, grains, and legumes! Here are some of the goitrogens you might come across:

- Glucosinolates: These compounds are mainly found in cruciferous veggies such as broccoli, cauliflower, Brussels sprouts, cabbage, and kale. They can play a role in messing with thyroid hormone production by blocking iodine absorption.

- Flavonoids: These compounds can be found in a range of plant-based foods, including soy and some tasty fruits! Flavonoids are packed with health benefits, but it's interesting to note that they can transform into goitrogenic substances during digestion!

- Thiocyanates: You can find these compounds in foods such as cassava, sweet potatoes, and some cruciferous vegetables! Thiocyanates can slow down the thyroid's ability to take in iodine, which can affect hormone production.

Getting to know the various types of goitrogens is super helpful! It sheds light on how they play with the thyroid and whether we should keep them in check or enjoy them in moderation in our meals. It's worth noting that goitrogens can have different effects on different people! For those with healthy thyroids, goitrogenic foods usually aren't a big concern! However, for those dealing with hypothyroidism or iodine deficiency, it's a good idea to be a bit more careful since their thyroid isn't quite up to speed.

Balancing Goitrogens in a Thyroid-Friendly Diet

Although the concept of goitrogens may seem a bit concerning, it's important to look at it with a well-rounded view. Lots of foods packed with goitrogens are actually super healthy and full of nutrients! Cruciferous vegetables are packed with vitamins, minerals, and antioxidants that boost overall health and help reduce inflammation—great news for thyroid function and your well-being! So, the aim isn't to completely cut these foods out of your diet, but rather to discover ways to lessen their goitrogenic effects and enjoy them in moderation.

One of the easiest ways to lessen the goitrogenic effects of certain foods is by simply cooking them. Cooking can reduce a good amount of the goitrogens present in raw cruciferous veggies, which means they're much less likely to mess with iodine absorption. For instance, giving vegetables like broccoli or kale a quick steam, a fun sauté, or a delightful roast can keep their nutritional perks intact while reducing their goitrogenic effects.

Another point to think about is iodine intake. For those with enough iodine, goitrogens aren't much of a concern at all! Incorporating iodine-rich foods like seaweed, seafood, and dairy into your diet can be a way to balance out the effects of goitrogens and give your thyroid the support it needs to thrive! It's important to keep in mind that if you're low on iodine, you might want to pay a bit more attention to your goitrogen intake, since not having enough iodine can make you more vulnerable to the downsides of these compounds.

Who Needs to Be Extra Careful with Goitrogens?

For the majority of people, particularly those who don't have a thyroid issue, goitrogens are really not something to worry about too much. For others, keeping an eye on goitrogenic foods can be quite helpful! People dealing with iodine deficiency, hypothyroidism, or Hashimoto's thyroiditis might want to think carefully about how frequently and in what ways they enjoy goitrogenic foods.

For instance, a person with hypothyroidism may benefit from cutting back on raw cruciferous veggies and opting for the cooked ones instead. In the same vein, individuals facing iodine deficiency should focus on incorporating iodine-rich foods into their meals and make sure their diet encourages healthy thyroid hormone production. Teaming up with a nutritionist or healthcare provider to find the perfect mix of goitrogenic and thyroid-friendly foods can lead to a delightful diet that caters to your body's unique needs, all while keeping things enjoyable and flexible!

Goitrogens in Context

It's so tempting to label foods as "good" or "bad" when thinking about health, but the reality is often a bit more nuanced! Goitrogens might sound a bit concerning for thyroid health in some people, but guess what? They're also present in many of the planet's healthiest foods! Finding the right balance between your goitrogenic food intake and your body's individual needs is the secret!

For many, including a mix of goitrogen-rich foods in a well-rounded, nutrient-packed diet is generally safe and worry-free! By keeping an eye on how you cook, your iodine intake, and the overall mix of your meals, you can enjoy the perks of these nutritious foods while reducing any potential effects of goitrogens.

In the end, a thriving thyroid is all about welcoming a balanced diet rather than steering clear of specific foods. It's about giving your body the nutrients it craves to work its best, while also being aware of any personal sensitivities or health concerns.

Inflammatory Foods and Thyroid Dysfunction

The link between inflammation and thyroid issues is profound and intricate. Chronic inflammation is a key player in the development and progression of various thyroid disorders, such as hypothyroidism and Hashimoto's thyroiditis, which is the most prevalent autoimmune thyroid condition. Inflammation is a natural immune response that helps protect the body, but when it sticks around for too long, it can start to harm healthy tissues, throw hormone production out of whack, and even spark autoimmune reactions. For those dealing with thyroid conditions, using diet to manage inflammation can be a fantastic way to enhance symptoms and promote lasting thyroid health.

This effort revolves around discovering the foods that spark inflammation and, on the flip side, those that can help calm it down. The contemporary Western diet is packed with inflammatory foods—often processed, refined, and loaded with added sugars, unhealthy fats, and artificial ingredients. For individuals with thyroid disorders, certain foods can really throw a wrench in the works, making symptoms like fatigue, weight gain, and brain fog even more challenging to manage.

Refined Sugars: Fuel for Inflammation

Refined sugars can be a major player in causing inflammation. Refined sugars are everywhere in our favorite processed foods, from fizzy drinks and tasty baked treats to flavorful sauces and condiments. They can cause our blood sugar levels to jump, which in turn triggers a boost in insulin production! As time goes on, this ongoing rollercoaster of blood sugar spikes and dips puts a strain on the body's metabolic system and sparks some inflammation throughout. The thyroid can be affected by inflammation, which throws hormone balance out of whack and can lead to weight gain, fatigue, and insulin resistance—challenges often faced by those dealing with hypothyroidism.

Additionally, indulging in too much sugar can spark an immune reaction that makes autoimmune thyroid conditions, such as Hashimoto's, even trickier to manage. When blood sugar levels rise, they can boost the production of cytokines, those little proteins that help manage inflammation. This can result in an overly enthusiastic immune system that might end up targeting thyroid tissue.

For a happy thyroid, cutting back on refined sugars is a key move! Choosing natural sweeteners like honey or maple syrup in moderation can lighten the inflammatory load while still keeping things sweet! Focusing on whole, nutrient-rich foods that help keep blood sugar steady—like complex carbs, healthy fats, and lean proteins—can really make a difference in reducing inflammation!

Processed Foods: A Recipe for Inflammation

Processed foods can really ramp up inflammation, mainly because they're packed with preservatives, additives, unhealthy fats, and refined sugars. These foods often lose their natural goodness and are packed with artificial ingredients that boost flavor, color, and shelf life instead. The body can sometimes have a tough time identifying and handling these artificial substances, which can spark an inflammatory immune response.

The types of fats found in processed foods can be quite tricky! Trans fats, those sneaky hydrogenated oils lurking in many fried and packaged goodies, can really stir up inflammation! These fats can boost levels of inflammatory markers in the body, like C-reactive protein (CRP), which tends to be higher in people with thyroid disorders. Elevated CRP levels can worsen symptoms and create challenges for the thyroid to operate effectively.

Plus, processed foods usually have a hefty dose of refined carbohydrates, which behave similarly to sugars in the body, causing blood glucose levels to soar and encouraging inflammation. These foods can spark inflammation and may also lead to weight gain and metabolic imbalances—two challenges often faced by those with thyroid issues.

Cutting back on processed foods can really boost your efforts in managing thyroid issues! Try to embrace whole, unprocessed foods like vegetables, fruits, lean proteins, and whole grains! These delicious options can help reduce inflammation and give your body the nutrients it craves for healing.

Gluten: A Trigger for Autoimmune Inflammation

For those dealing with Hashimoto's thyroiditis, gluten can be quite the troublemaker when it comes to inflammation. Gluten is a protein that pops up in wheat, barley, and rye, and for some people, especially those with certain autoimmune conditions, it can stir up an immune reaction! Studies indicate a notable connection between gluten sensitivity and autoimmune thyroid disease, with some people noticing a decrease in thyroid antibodies and an enhancement in symptoms after switching to a gluten-free diet.

For those with gluten sensitivity or celiac disease, gluten can harm the gut lining, leading to what's known as leaky gut syndrome. This condition lets undigested food particles, toxins, and pathogens sneak into the bloodstream, sparking an immune response that can ramp up thyroid inflammation and intensify autoimmune attacks on the thyroid gland.

Many people with thyroid disorders, have found that embracing a gluten-free diet can be a fantastic approach! Removing gluten allows the gut to start its healing journey, helping to lower inflammation and soothe the immune system's response towards the thyroid. If you're thinking about this approach, it's important to emphasize whole, naturally gluten-free foods like fruits, vegetables, lean proteins, and gluten-free grains such as quinoa and rice. Steering clear of processed gluten-free products is a good idea, as they can be just as inflammatory as those containing gluten.

Dairy: A Potential Inflammatory Food for Some

Dairy products are packed with calcium and other nutrients, but they can be a bit tricky for some people, especially those who are lactose intolerant or sensitive to casein, the protein in milk. Dairy sensitivities might cause some digestive discomfort, a bit of extra mucus, and even some inflammation, which can put a extra pressure on the thyroid.

If you have thyroid disorders and often deal with digestive troubles, cutting back on dairy could be a way to help ease inflammation and boost your thyroid health! Almond milk, coconut milk, are fantastic non-dairy alternatives that offer a delightful substitute without causing any inflammatory effects. It's a good idea to pick unsweetened, minimally processed options to keep sugar and other inflammatory ingredients out of your diet.

Artificial Additives: Hidden Inflammatory Triggers

When managing thyroid dysfunction, it's a good idea to steer clear of foods packed with artificial additives, like food dyes, preservatives, and artificial sweeteners. These substances can sneak into processed foods, drinks, and snacks, and they might play a role in causing systemic inflammation and metabolic disruption.

Artificial sweeteners can shake things up in the body's natural metabolic dance, sometimes causing those cravings to pop up, contributing to insulin resistance, and sparking inflammatory reactions. If you're navigating thyroid disorders, steering clear of products with additives can lighten the inflammatory load on your body, helping your thyroid to work its magic more smoothly!

A Thyroid-Friendly Approach to Reducing Inflammation

By concentrating on cutting back or removing inflammatory foods such as refined sugars, processed items, gluten, dairy (for those who are sensitive), and artificial additives, people with thyroid issues can foster a setting where their thyroid can thrive and operate more efficiently. Cutting down on inflammation is a win-win! It not only helps the thyroid but also boosts your whole body, enhancing your energy, sharpening your mind, and uplifting your overall wellness.

The most effective way to tackle inflammation is by focusing on whole, nutrient-packed foods that are bursting with antioxidants, healthy fats, and fiber—foods that calm inflammation instead of igniting it. As you embrace these changes, you might see some wonderful improvements in your thyroid health and your overall quality of life!

Chapter 5: Breakfast Recipes

Starting your day on the right foot can truly set the tone for everything that follows! For those navigating thyroid health challenges, breakfast isn't just the first meal of the day—it's a golden opportunity to nourish your body with the ideal balance of macronutrients. Think of it as your morning fuel: proteins to repair and build, healthy fats to support hormone production, and complex carbohydrates to provide lasting energy. But it's not just about macronutrients; it's also about packing in the vitamins and minerals your thyroid relies on to function at its best, like selenium, iodine, magnesium, and more. A thoughtfully crafted breakfast doesn't just steady your energy levels—it jump-starts your metabolism, supports mental clarity, and gives you a vibrant boost to tackle the day ahead.

Get ready to treat yourself to thyroid-loving breakfasts that are as wholesome as they are delicious! From creamy, nutrient-packed smoothies bursting with flavor to warm and comforting bowls packed with fiber and antioxidants, these recipes are designed to energize you and set the stage for a productive, feel-good day. Whatever your morning style, these thyroid-friendly options will leave you satisfied, uplifted, and ready to take on anything!

1. Avocado & Spinach Smoothie

This creamy, nutrient-packed smoothie is loaded with healthy fats, fiber, and a blend of vitamins and minerals that support thyroid function. Avocado provides a dose of selenium, while spinach gives you a boost of iron and magnesium.

Prep Time: 5 minutes
Cooking Time: None
Servings: 1

Ingredients:
- ½ ripe avocado
- 1 cup fresh spinach
- 1 tablespoon chia seeds
- 1 cup unsweetened almond milk
- 1 teaspoon honey (optional)
- 1 tablespoon flaxseed oil
- Ice cubes (optional)

Instructions:
1. Place all ingredients in a blender and blend until smooth.
2. Add more almond milk if the consistency is too thick.
3. Serve immediately.

Nutritional Info (Per Serving):

Calories: 350 kcal per serving

Fats: 28 g (3.5 g saturated)

Carbohydrates: 15 g (8 g fiber, 6 g sugar)

Protein: 6 g

Key Nutrients: Rich in selenium, magnesium, and omega-3 fatty acids, with high amounts of fiber and healthy monounsaturated fats.

Tips: To enhance the creaminess, use frozen avocado or spinach. Add a pinch of cinnamon for extra flavor and potential blood sugar regulation.

2. Berry Coconut Yogurt Bowl

This yogurt bowl is a refreshing and satisfying breakfast full of antioxidants, healthy fats, and probiotics. The mixed berries and banana provide a burst of vitamins, while the coconut flakes add texture and healthy fats to nourish your thyroid.

Prep Time: 5 minutes
Cooking Time: None
Servings: 1

Ingredients:
- 1 cup unsweetened coconut yogurt
- ½ cup mixed berries (blueberries, raspberries, strawberries)
- 1 sliced banana
- 1 tablespoon chia seeds
- 2 tablespoons unsweetened shredded coconut
- 1 tablespoon pumpkin seeds
- Drizzle of honey (optional)

Instructions:
1. In a bowl, add the coconut yogurt.
2. Top with mixed berries, sliced banana, chia seeds, shredded coconut, and pumpkin seeds.
3. Drizzle with honey, if desired.

Nutritional Info (Per Serving):

Calories: 310 kcal per serving

Fats: 18 g (12 g saturated)
Carbohydrates: 22 g (6 g fiber, 14 g sugar)
Protein: 8 g

Key Nutrients: Contains antioxidants (vitamin C), healthy fats from coconut, and probiotics for gut health.

Tips: Substitute pumpkin seeds with sunflower seeds for a different crunch. Use fresh seasonal berries for the best flavor and nutrient density.

3. Delicious Breakfast Omelette

This steamy, freshly cooked omelette is filled with juicy tomatoes and green onions, providing a nutrient-packed start to your day. Served with crispy potatoes on the side, it offers a satisfying combination of protein, fiber, and healthy fats.

Prep Time: 10 minutes
Cooking Time: 15 minutes
Servings: 1

Ingredients:
- 3 large eggs
- 1 tablespoon olive oil
- 1 medium potato, diced
- ½ tomato, diced
- 2 tablespoons chopped green onions
- 1 tablespoon fresh parsley, chopped (optional)
- Salt and pepper to taste

Instructions:
1. Cook the potatoes: Heat half of the olive oil in a skillet over medium heat. Add the diced potatoes and cook until golden brown and crispy, about 10-12 minutes. Stir occasionally and season with salt and pepper. Remove from the skillet and set aside.
2. Make the omelette: In the same skillet, heat the remaining olive oil over medium heat. Whisk the eggs in a small bowl, season with salt and pepper, and pour into the pan. Let the eggs set for about 2 minutes.
3. Add toppings: Sprinkle the diced tomatoes and chopped green onions over the omelette. Cook for another 2-3 minutes, folding the omelette over once the edges are firm.
4. Serve the omelette with the crispy potatoes on the side and garnish with fresh parsley if desired.

Nutritional Info (Per Serving):
Calories: 413 kcal per serving
Fats: 25 g (6 g saturated)
Carbohydrates: 29 g (4 g fiber, 2 g sugar)
Protein: 18 g

Key Nutrients: High in protein, iron, vitamin A, and potassium, with fiber from potatoes and tomatoes.

Tips: Experiment with other vegetables like bell peppers or zucchini. Adding a pinch of turmeric can provide additional anti-inflammatory benefits.

4. Chia Seed Pudding with Sliced Almonds

This chia seed pudding is packed with fiber, omega-3s, and healthy fats. It's easy to prepare the night before, making it a perfect grab-and-go breakfast.

Prep Time: 5 minutes
Cooking Time: None (requires 4+ hours refrigeration)
Servings: 1

Ingredients:
- 3 tablespoons chia seeds
- 1 cup unsweetened almond milk
- 1 teaspoon vanilla extract
- 1 handful of sliced almonds
- 1 teaspoon maple syrup
- Fresh berries for topping

Instructions:
1. In a bowl, mix chia seeds, almond milk, vanilla extract, and maple syrup. Stir well.
2. Refrigerate overnight, or for at least 4 hours, until the mixture thickens into a pudding consistency.
3. Before serving, top with sliced almonds and fresh berries.

Nutritional Info (Per Serving):
Calories: 280 kcal per serving
Fats: 18 g (2 g saturated)
Carbohydrates: 18 g (9 g fiber, 7 g sugar)
Protein: 9 g

Key Nutrients: High in omega-3 fatty acids, calcium, fiber, and plant-based protein.

Tips: Use canned coconut milk for a creamier texture. Stir the mixture after an hour to ensure even hydration of chia seeds.

5. Protein-Packed Green Smoothie

This smoothie combines whey isolate protein powder with a dose of thyroid-supporting vitamins and minerals. It's light but energizing—perfect for busy mornings.

Prep Time: 5 minutes
Cooking Time: None
Servings: 1

Ingredients:
- 1 scoop whey isolate protein powder
- 1 cup unsweetened coconut water
- ½ banana
- 1 cup fresh spinach
- 1 tablespoon chia seeds
- 1 teaspoon spirulina powder
- Ice cubes

Instructions:
1. Add all ingredients to a blender and blend until smooth.
2. Serve immediately.

Nutritional Info (Per Serving):
Calories: 270 kcal per serving
Fats: 12 g (2.5 g saturated)
Carbohydrates: 21 g (6 g fiber, 8 g sugar)
Protein: 19 g

Key Nutrients: Excellent source of protein, vitamin B12, iron, and chlorophyll, with additional electrolytes from coconut water.

Tips: Use frozen spinach for a nutrient-dense boost and chillier smoothie. A few drops of vanilla extract can enhance the flavor.

6. Oatmeal with Walnuts & Blueberries

Oats are a great source of complex carbohydrates and fiber, helping to keep blood sugar levels stable throughout the morning. Rich in selenium from walnuts and antioxidants from blueberries, this meal supports thyroid function and provides stable energy.

Prep Time: 5 minutes
Cooking Time: 5 minutes
Servings: 1

Ingredients:
- ½ cup rolled oats
- 1 cup water or unsweetened almond milk
- 1 tablespoon chopped walnuts
- ½ cup fresh blueberries
- 1 teaspoon cinnamon
- Drizzle of maple syrup (optional)

Instructions:
1. Cook oats in water or almond milk according to package instructions.
2. Once cooked, stir in cinnamon and top with walnuts and blueberries.
3. Drizzle with maple syrup, if desired.

Nutritional Info (Per Serving):
Calories: 320 kcal per serving
Fats: 12 g (1.5 g saturated)
Carbohydrates: 45 g (6 g fiber, 8 g sugar)
Protein: 7 g

Key Nutrients: High in selenium, manganese, fiber, and antioxidants (vitamin C and polyphenols).

Tips: To save time in the morning, you can soak the oats overnight and cook them quickly in the morning. Add a pinch of sea salt to enhance the flavor.

7. Ground Grass-fed Beef with Bell Peppers and Onions

This savory scramble features ground grass-fed beef paired with vibrant bell peppers and onions, offering a boost of protein, vitamins, and healthy fats. Packed with zinc and selenium from the beef and vitamin C from the bell peppers, this dish helps maintain a healthy thyroid and supports overall immunity.

Prep Time: 10 minutes
Cooking Time: 10 minutes
Servings: 1

Ingredients:
- 200g ground grass-fed beef
- 1 tablespoon olive oil
- 1 cup diced bell peppers (red, yellow, green)
- 1 onion, sliced
- 1 teaspoon turmeric
- Salt and pepper to taste

Instructions:
1. Cook the beef: Heat olive oil in a pan over medium heat. Add the ground beef, season with turmeric, salt, and pepper, and cook for about 5-7 minutes until browned.
2. Sauté the bell peppers and onions: Add the diced bell peppers and onions to the pan and cook for 3-4 minutes, until they soften but still retain a bit of crunch.
3. Serve the beef with the bell peppers and onions.

Nutritional Info (Per Serving):
Calories: 698 kcal per serving
Fats: 50 g (15 g saturated)
Carbohydrates: 12 g (3 g fiber, 6 g sugar)
Protein: 50 g

Key Nutrients: High in zinc, selenium, iron, vitamin C, and beta-carotene.

Tips: Use pre-cut vegetables to save time, serve with a side of avocado for added healthy fats.

8. Coconut Flour Pancakes

Coconut flour provides fiber and healthy fats that nourish the thyroid, while eggs add selenium and protein.

Prep Time: 5 minutes
Cooking Time: 6 minutes
Servings: 1

Ingredients:
- ¼ cup coconut flour
- 2 eggs
- ¼ cup unsweetened almond milk
- 1 teaspoon vanilla extract
- ½ teaspoon baking powder
- Coconut oil for cooking
- Drizzle of maple syrup
- Fresh berries for topping

Instructions:
1. Mix coconut flour, eggs, almond milk, vanilla, and baking powder until smooth.
2. Heat coconut oil in a skillet and pour batter to form small pancakes.
3. Cook for 2-3 minutes on each side until golden brown.
4. Top with fresh berries and a drizzle of maple syrup and serve.

Nutritional Info (Per Serving):
Calories: 320 kcal per serving
Fats: 24 g (5 g saturated)
Carbohydrates: 12 g (5 g fiber, 4 g sugar)
Protein: 10 g

Key Nutrients: High in selenium, lauric acid, fiber, and vitamin B12.

Tips: Use a small skillet to ensure even cooking, and make a double batch to freeze extras for later. Warm them up in the toaster for a quick breakfast.

9. Egg & Avocado Toast on Gluten-Free Bread

The combination of eggs and avocado on a gluten-free bread base delivers selenium, healthy fats, and vitamin E, which are beneficial for thyroid health.

Prep Time: 5 minutes
Cooking Time: 3 minutes
Servings: 1

Ingredients:
- 1 slice gluten-free bread, toasted
- ½ avocado, mashed
- 1 large egg, fried or poached
- Pinch of red pepper flakes
- Salt and pepper to taste

Instructions:
1. Spread mashed avocado on the toasted gluten-free bread.
2. Top with a fried or poached egg.
3. Season with red pepper flakes, salt, and pepper.

Nutritional Info (Per Serving):
Calories: 290 kcal per serving
Fats: 19 g (4 g saturated)
Carbohydrates: 20 g (5 g fiber, 3 g sugar)
Protein: 11 g

Key Nutrients: High in selenium, potassium, vitamin E, and monounsaturated fats.

Tips: Use a ripe avocado for easy mashing.

10. Quinoa Breakfast Bowl with Almonds & Berries

Quinoa is a complete protein and rich in magnesium, while berries and almonds provide antioxidants and selenium to support thyroid health.

Prep Time: 5 minutes
Cooking Time: 5 minutes (if quinoa is pre-cooked)
Servings: 1

Ingredients:
- ½ cup cooked quinoa
- ¼ cup fresh berries
- 1 tablespoon chopped almonds
- 1 tablespoon chia seeds
- ½ cup unsweetened almond milk
- Drizzle of honey (optional)

Instructions:
1. Combine quinoa, berries, almonds, and chia seeds in a bowl.
2. Pour almond milk over the mixture and drizzle with honey.

Nutritional Info (Per Serving):
Calories: 310 kcal per serving
Fats: 14 g (1.5 g saturated)
Carbohydrates: 37 g (8 g fiber, 12 g sugar)
Protein: 9 g

Key Nutrients: High in magnesium, selenium, fiber, and antioxidants (vitamin C and flavonoids).

Tips: Cook quinoa in advance and store it in the fridge for quick assembly. Add a sprinkle of cinnamon for extra flavor and blood sugar control.

11. Smoked Salmon, Scramble Eggs & Avocado

This dish is rich in iodine and selenium from eggs and smoked salmon, plus omega-3 fatty acids and magnesium from avocado, making it a nutrient powerhouse for thyroid health.

Prep Time: 5 minutes
Cooking Time: 5 minutes
Servings: 1

Ingredients:
- 2 large eggs
- 1 slice smoked salmon, chopped
- 1/2 sliced avocado
- cherry tomatoes
- 1 tablespoon olive oil
- Salt and pepper to taste

Instructions:
1. Heat olive oil in a pan, add eggs and scramble lightly.
3. Toss in the smoked salmon and cook for 1-2 minutes.
4. Season with salt and pepper.
5. Serve with cherry tomatoes and sliced avocado.

Nutritional Info (Per Serving):
Calories: 500 kcal per serving
Fats: 35 g (6 g saturated)
Carbohydrates: 11 g (4 g fiber, 2 g sugar)
Protein: 35 g

Key Nutrients: High in omega-3 fatty acids, selenium, iodine, magnesium, and vitamin D.

Tips: Use a non-stick pan to prevent the eggs from sticking and avoid overcooking the salmon to maintain its tender texture. Pair with a slice of gluten-free toast for added fiber.

12. Chia & Almond Butter Smoothie

This smoothie provides magnesium, fiber, and healthy fats from chia seeds and almond butter, promoting thyroid function and keeping you energized.

Prep Time: 2 minutes
Cooking Time: None
Servings: 1

Ingredients:
- 1 tablespoon chia seeds
- 1 tablespoon almond butter
- 1 cup unsweetened almond milk
- ½ banana
- 1 teaspoon honey (optional)
- Ice cubes

Instructions:
1. Blend all ingredients together until smooth.
2. Serve chilled.

Nutritional Info (Per Serving):
Calories: 270 kcal per serving
Fats: 16 g (2 g saturated)
Carbohydrates: 24 g (5 g fiber, 11 g sugar)
Protein: 7 g

Key Nutrients: Rich in magnesium, fiber, vitamin E, and omega-3 fatty acids.

Tips: Use frozen banana slices for a creamier texture, and adjust the thickness by adding more or less almond milk. Perfect for a quick breakfast on the go.

13. Coconut Yogurt Bowl with Nuts and Berries

Packed with selenium from nuts, antioxidants from berries, and probiotics from coconut yogurt, this bowl supports thyroid health and digestion.

Prep Time: 5 minutes
Cooking Time: None
Servings: 1

Ingredients:
- ¾ cup coconut yogurt
- 2 tablespoons mixed nuts (almonds, walnuts)
- 1 tablespoon sunflower seeds
- 1 cup berries
- Drizzle of honey (eventual)

Instructions:
1. In a bowl, layer coconut yogurt, nuts, seeds, and berries.
2. Drizzle honey over the top and serve.

Nutritional Info (Per Serving):
Calories: 350 kcal per serving
Fats: 22 g (8 g saturated)
Carbohydrates: 20 g (6 g fiber, 9 g sugar)
Protein: 19 g

Key Nutrients: High in selenium, vitamin C, antioxidants, and healthy fats.

Tips: Use a mix of seasonal berries for a variety of flavors and nutrients. Add a sprinkle of cinnamon for a natural boost in blood sugar control.

14. Quinoa Porridge with Apple, Banana and Berries

Quinoa provides plant-based protein, while the fruits contribute antioxidants and essential vitamins to support thyroid and immune health.

Prep Time: 5 minutes
Cooking Time: 7 minutes
Servings: 1

Ingredients:
- ½ cup quinoa flakes
- 1 cup unsweetened almond milk
- 1 small apple, diced
- ½ banana
- handful of berries
- Drizzle of maple syrup (eventual)

Instructions:
1. Combine cooked quinoa flakes, almond milk, and apple in a saucepan. Simmer for 5-7 minutes.
2. Add sliced banana, sliced apple and berries.
3. Drizzle with maple syrup (eventual) and serve.

Nutritional Info (Per Serving):
Calories: 310 kcal per serving
Fats: 10 g (2 g saturated)
Carbohydrates: 50 g (7 g fiber, 20 g sugar)
Protein: 7 g

Key Nutrients: High in magnesium, vitamin C, fiber, and antioxidants.

Tips: Use pre-cooked quinoa flakes to reduce preparation time. Top with a dash of nutmeg for an extra warm and spiced flavor.

15. Breakfast Bowl with Poached Egg, Quinoa, Avocado, Cherry Tomatoes, and Pesto

Combining selenium and protein from eggs, magnesium from quinoa, and healthy fats from avocado and pesto, this bowl is designed to nourish thyroid function and boost overall wellness.

Prep Time: 10 minutes
Cooking Time: 10 minutes
Servings: 1

Ingredients:
- ½ cup cooked quinoa
- 1 large egg
- ½ avocado, sliced
- 6-8 cherry tomatoes, halved
- 1 tablespoon pesto sauce (homemade or store-bought)
- 1 teaspoon olive oil (for poaching)
- Salt and pepper to taste
- Fresh basil leaves (optional for garnish)

Instructions:
1. Cook the quinoa: Prepare the quinoa according to package instructions, then set aside to cool slightly.
2. Poach the egg: Bring a small saucepan of water to a gentle simmer and add 1 teaspoon of olive oil. Crack the egg into a small bowl, then gently slide it into the water. Poach for about 3-4 minutes until the white is set but the yolk is still runny. Remove with a slotted spoon and set aside.
3. Assemble the bowl: In a serving bowl, place the cooked quinoa at the base. Arrange the sliced avocado and halved cherry tomatoes around the quinoa.
4. Top with the egg: Gently place the poached egg on top of the quinoa and vegetables.
5. Add pesto: Drizzle the pesto sauce over the bowl and season with salt and pepper to taste.
6. Garnish with fresh basil leaves if desired.

Nutritional Info (Per Serving):
Calories: 420 kcal per serving
Fats: 27 g (4.5 g saturated)
Carbohydrates: 30 g (7 g fiber, 5 g sugar)
Protein: 16 g

Key Nutrients: High in selenium, magnesium, omega-3 fatty acids, and vitamin C.

Tips: Use leftover cooked quinoa for an even faster assembly. Add a squeeze of lemon over the bowl for a fresh citrus kick and extra vitamin C.

Chapter 6: Lunch Recipes

Lunch is the perfect opportunity to fuel your body with a delicious and balanced meal that not only satisfies your hunger but also keeps your thyroid thriving. This essential mid-day meal sets the tone for sustained energy and focus throughout the day, making it all the more important to choose nutrient-packed dishes. These recipes celebrate whole, nutrient-dense ingredients that are easy to digest and packed with vital nutrients like selenium, iodine, and healthy fats, all of which are key to supporting thyroid health and overall well-being.

Whether you're craving a vibrant grain bowl filled with fluffy basmati rice, a hearty soup bursting with wholesome vegetables, or a refreshing salad paired with perfectly grilled protein, these recipes are designed to nourish and delight. They bring together fresh flavors, vibrant colors, and rich textures to create meals that are as satisfying to eat as they are beneficial for your health. With each bite, you'll be giving your thyroid—and your body—the care it deserves. Get ready to embrace lunch as a chance to refuel and recharge with these flavorful, thyroid-friendly creations!

1. Grilled Chicken Bowl with White Rice and Avocado

This bowl combines lean protein, selenium-rich avocado, and energy-boosting white rice, which provides easily digestible carbs essential for thyroid support.

Prep time: 10 minutes
Cooking time: 15 minutes
Servings: 2

Ingredients:
- 1 cup cooked white rice
- 1 grilled chicken breast, sliced
- ½ avocado, sliced
- 1 tablespoon olive oil
- 1 tablespoon lemon juice
- cherry tomatoes
- 1 tablespoon fresh parsley, chopped
- Salt and pepper to taste

Instructions:
1. Arrange the cooked basmati rice in a bowl. Top with sliced grilled chicken, avocado and cherry tomatoes.
2. Drizzle with olive oil and lemon juice, sprinkle with fresh parsley, and season with salt and pepper.

Nutritional Info (Per serving):
Calories: 450 kcal per serving
Fats: 20 g (3 g saturated)
Carbohydrates: 40 g (3 g fiber, 2 g sugar)
Protein: 28 g

Key nutrients: Selenium (from avocado), potassium, vitamin B6, and magnesium

Tips: Add a sprinkle of chili flakes for a touch of heat or a side of leafy greens for added fiber.

2. Shrimp and Basmati Rice Bowl with Steamed Vegetables

Shrimp is rich in iodine, while the colorful steamed vegetables add antioxidants and essential nutrients that support thyroid function.

Prep time: 10 minutes
Cooking time: 15 minutes
Servings: 2

Ingredients:
- 1 cup cooked basmati rice
- 100g shrimp, peeled and deveined
- 1 cup steamed peas, bell peppers and carrots (or other veggies of your choice)
- 1 tablespoon olive oil
- Salt and pepper to taste

Instructions:
1. Sauté shrimp in olive oil until cooked through, about 3-4 minutes.
2. Steam vegetables until tender.
3. Serve shrimp and vegetables over cooked basmati rice, drizzle with olive oil, and season with salt and pepper.

Nutritional Info (Per Serving):
Calories: 420 kcal per serving
Fats: 16 g (2.5 g saturated)
Carbohydrates: 45 g (5 g fiber, 6 g sugar)
Protein: 25 g

Key nutrients: Iodine (from shrimp), vitamin C, beta-carotene, and magnesium

Tips: For added flavor, sprinkle with sesame seeds before serving.

3. Grilled Turkey with Quinoa, Broccoli, and Bell Peppers

Turkey provides lean protein, while broccoli and quinoa offer fiber, selenium, and magnesium essential for optimal thyroid health.

Prep time: 15 minutes
Cooking time: 25 minutes
Servings: 2

Ingredients:
- 100g turkey breast, boneless
- 1 cup cooked quinoa
- 1 cup broccoli florets
- ½ red bell pepper, sliced
- ½ yellow bell pepper, sliced
- 1 tablespoon olive oil
- 1 teaspoon garlic powder
- 1 teaspoon paprika
- Salt and pepper to taste
- 1 tablespoon fresh parsley, chopped (optional)

Instructions:

1. Prepare the turkey:
   - Preheat the grill to medium-high heat.
   - Rub the turkey breast with olive oil, garlic powder, paprika, salt, and pepper.
   - Grill the turkey breast for 5-7 minutes on each side, or until fully cooked. Remove from the grill and let it rest for a few minutes before slicing.

2. Cook the quinoa:
   - If you haven't cooked the quinoa yet, rinse ½ cup of dry quinoa under cold water.
   - Add the quinoa and 1 cup of water to a pot and bring to a boil.
   - Once boiling, reduce the heat, cover, and simmer for 15 minutes or until the water is absorbed. Fluff with a fork and set aside.

3. Roast the vegetables:
   - Preheat your oven to 400°F (200°C).
   - Toss the broccoli florets and sliced bell peppers with 1 teaspoon of olive oil, salt, and pepper.
   - Spread the vegetables on a baking sheet and roast for 15-20 minutes, until tender and slightly caramelized.

4. Assemble the meal:
   - Serve the grilled turkey breast slices alongside the cooked quinoa.
   - Arrange the roasted broccoli and bell peppers on the plate.
   - Optionally, garnish with fresh parsley for a touch of color and extra flavor.

Nutritional Info (Per Serving):
Calories: 450 kcal per serving
Fats: 18 g (3 g saturated)
Carbohydrates: 42 g (7 g fiber, 5 g sugar)
Protein: 35 g

Key nutrients: Selenium, iron (from turkey and quinoa), folate, vitamin C, and zinc

Tips: Add a squeeze of fresh lemon juice over the turkey for extra zest or sprinkle with nutritional yeast for a cheesy flavor.

4. Salmon Sushi Rice Bowl with Cucumber and Avocado

Salmon is rich in omega-3 fatty acids and iodine, while avocado adds selenium and healthy fats that support thyroid health.

Prep time: 10 minutes
Cooking time: 10 minutes (if rice isn't cooked already)
Servings: 2

Ingredients:
- 1 cup cooked basmati rice
- 100g sashimi salmon
- ½ cucumber, sliced
- ½ avocado, sliced
- 1 tablespoon olive oil
- 1 tablespoon lemon juice
- Salt and pepper to taste
- 1 tablespoon wasabi

Instructions:
1. Arrange cooked basmati rice in a bowl. Top with sashimi salmon, sliced cucumber, and avocado.
2. Drizzle with olive oil and lemon juice, and season with salt and pepper.
3. Add a tablespoon of wasabi.

Nutritional Info (Per Serving):
Calories: 470 kcal per serving
Fats: 25 g (4 g saturated)
Carbohydrates: 40 g (5 g fiber, 3 g sugar)
Protein: 28 g

Key nutrients: Omega-3 fatty acids, iodine, selenium, potassium, and vitamin E

Tips: Garnish with nori strips or sesame seeds for extra flavor and a boost of nutrients.

5. Lentil and Spinach Soup with Fresh Herbs

Lentils provide plant-based protein and iron, while spinach adds magnesium and selenium, making this soup an excellent thyroid-nourishing meal.

Prep time: 10 minutes
Cooking time: 15 minutes
Servings: 3

Ingredients:
- 1 cup green lentils, cooked
- 2 cups vegetable broth
- 1 cup fresh spinach
- 1 small onion, chopped
- 1 tablespoon olive oil
- 1 teaspoon cumin
- 1 tablespoon chopped fresh parsley
- Salt and pepper to taste

Instructions:
1. Heat olive oil in a pot over medium heat. Sauté onion until translucent.
2. Add vegetable broth, cooked lentils, cumin, and spinach. Simmer for 10 minutes.
3. Stir in parsley, season with salt and pepper, and serve hot.

Nutritional Info (Per Serving):
Calories: 360 kcal per serving
Fats: 9 g (1.5 g saturated)
Carbohydrates: 52 g (10 g fiber, 6 g sugar)
Protein: 17 g

Key nutrients: Iron (from lentils), magnesium, folate, selenium, and potassium

Tips: Add a squeeze of lemon juice for added richness and brightness.

6. Mediterranean Salad

Sardines are rich in iodine and omega-3 fatty acids, which are essential for maintaining thyroid health.

Prep time: 10 minutes
Cooking time: None
Servings: 2

Ingredients:

- 2 fillets of marinated sardines (fresh or canned in olive oil)

- 1 small cucumber, thinly sliced

- ½ red onion, thinly sliced

- 1 celery stalk, sliced

- 1 tablespoon capers, drained

- Fresh dill, for garnish

- 1 tablespoon extra-virgin olive oil

- Juice of ½ lemon

- Salt and black pepper to taste

- 2 slices of gluten-free bread (toasted)

- Mixed greens (optional)

Instructions:
1. In a medium bowl, combine the sliced cucumber, red onion, and celery. Add the capers and drizzle with olive oil and lemon juice. Toss gently to coat.

2. Place the marinated sardine fillets on top of the salad mixture and season with salt and black pepper.

3. Garnish with fresh dill and serve the salad alongside toasted gluten-free bread.

4. Optionally, you can add a handful of mixed greens for extra freshness and nutrients.

Nutritional Info (Per Serving):

Calories: 280 kcal per serving

Fats: 18 g (4 g saturated)

Carbohydrates: 20 g (5 g fiber, 3 g sugar)

Protein: 15 g

Key nutrients: Omega-3 fatty acids, iodine, vitamin C (from vegetables), and magnesium

Tips: Add a drizzle of balsamic glaze for extra sweetness.

7. Chicken and Basmati Rice Bowl with cucumbers, tomatoes and olives

The combination of lean protein, healthy fats, and nutrient-rich vegetables provides a balanced meal that supports overall thyroid function.

Prep time: 10 minutes
Cooking time: 15 minutes
Servings: 2

Ingredients:
- 1 grilled chicken breast, sliced into strips
- 1 cup cooked basmati rice
- 1 cup cucumber, sliced
- 1 cup cherry tomatoes, halved
- ¼ cup Kalamata olives, halved
- 2 tablespoons extra virgin olive oil
- 1 tablespoon lemon juice
- fresh rosemary
- Salt and pepper to taste
- Fresh rosemary for garnish

Instructions:
1. Grill the chicken:
   - Preheat your grill to medium-high heat.
   - Season the chicken breast with salt, pepper, and rosemary.
   - Grill the chicken for about 5-7 minutes on each side until fully cooked. Remove from the grill and slice into strips.

2. Prepare the vegetables:
   - In a large bowl, combine the sliced cucumber, halved cherry tomatoes, and Kalamata olives.
   - Drizzle with olive oil and lemon juice. Season with salt, pepper, and additional oregano if desired. Toss to coat the vegetables evenly.

3. Assemble the bowl:
   - In a rustic ceramic bowl, layer the cooked basmati rice and fresh vegetable mixture.
   - Add the grilled chicken strips on top.
   - Garnish with fresh rosemary for a burst of color and extra flavor.

Nutritional Info (Per Serving):
Calories: 420 kcal per serving
Fats: 28 g (5 g saturated)
Carbohydrates: 10 g (2 g fiber, 3 g sugar)
Protein: 30 g

Key nutrients: Selenium (from chicken), potassium, vitamin C, and magnesium

Tips: For a tangy twist, add a sprinkle of sumac on top.

8. Turkey Curry with Basmati Rice

Turkey is an excellent source of lean protein and selenium, while the curry spices promote anti-inflammatory benefits.

Prep time: 10 minutes
Cooking time: 40 minutes
Servings: 4

Ingredients:
- **For the turkey curry:**
  - 500g turkey breast, cubed
  - 1 tablespoon olive oil
  - 1 onion, chopped
  - 1 red bell pepper, diced
  - 1 yellow bell pepper, diced
  - 2 medium potatoes, peeled and cubed
  - 2 cloves garlic, minced
  - 1 tablespoon curry powder
  - 1 teaspoon ground cumin
  - 1 teaspoon ground turmeric
  - 1 can (400ml) coconut milk
  - 1 cup diced tomatoes (fresh or canned)
  - Salt and pepper to taste
  - Fresh cilantro for garnish
- **For the rice:**
  - 1 cup basmati rice
  - 2 cups water
  - Salt to taste
- Lemon wedges for serving

Instructions:

1. Cook the rice:
   - Rinse the basmati rice under cold water until the water runs clear.
   - In a medium pot, combine the rice, water, and a pinch of salt. Bring to a boil, then reduce the heat to low, cover, and simmer for 15 minutes, or until the water is absorbed and the rice is tender. Fluff with a fork and set aside.

2. Cook the turkey curry:
   - Heat olive oil in a large pan over medium heat. Add the cubed turkey and cook for about 5-7 minutes until browned on all sides. Remove from the pan and set aside.

- In the same pan, add chopped onion and minced garlic. Sauté for 3-4 minutes until softened.
- Add the diced bell peppers and cubed potatoes, and sauté for another 5 minutes.
- Stir in the curry powder, cumin, turmeric, and diced tomatoes. Cook for 2 minutes until fragrant.
- Pour in the coconut milk and return the turkey to the pan. Season with salt and pepper to taste.
- Simmer the curry for 20-25 minutes, stirring occasionally, until the potatoes are tender and the turkey is cooked through. The sauce should thicken slightly.

3. Assemble and garnish:
- Serve the turkey curry with basmati rice.
- Garnish with fresh cilantro and a squeeze of lemon juice from lemon wedges for added brightness.

Nutritional Info (Per Serving) :
Calories: 540 kcal per serving
Fats: 22 g (8 g saturated)
Carbohydrates: 55 g (6 g fiber, 8 g sugar)
Protein: 32 g

Key nutrients: Selenium, vitamin C (from bell peppers), beta-carotene, and zinc

Tips: Serve with gluten-free naan bread for a heartier meal.

9. Savory Sunday Lunch with Shredded Beef, Rice and Fried Plantains

The combination of slow-cooked beef and plantains provides iron and complex carbohydrates, essential for thyroid hormone production and energy metabolism.

Prep time: 15 minutes
Cooking time: 3 hours
Servings: 4

Ingredients:
- **For the beef:**
  - 500g beef chuck roast (or flank steak)
  - 1 large onion, diced
  - 1 red bell pepper, diced
  - 2 cloves garlic, minced
  - 1 teaspoon cumin
  - 1 teaspoon smoked paprika
  - 1 teaspoon oregano
  - 1 tablespoon tomato paste
  - 1 cup beef broth
  - 2 tablespoons olive oil
  - Salt and pepper to taste
- **For the rice:**
  - 1 cup white rice (Basmati or long-grain)
  - 2 cups water
  - Salt to taste
- **For the plantains:**
  - 1 ripe plantain, sliced
  - 2 tablespoons olive oil (for frying)
  - Salt to taste
- Fresh parsley or cilantro for garnish

Instructions:

1. Cook the beef:
   - Heat 2 tablespoons of olive oil in a large pot or Dutch oven over medium heat.
   - Season the beef with salt and pepper, then sear on all sides until browned (about 3-4 minutes per side). Remove the beef from the pot and set aside.
   - In the same pot, add diced onion, red bell pepper, and garlic. Sauté until softened, about 5 minutes.

- Stir in cumin, smoked paprika, oregano, and tomato paste. Cook for another 2 minutes.
   - Add beef broth and return the seared beef to the pot. Cover and simmer on low heat for 2-3 hours, or until the beef is tender and can be easily shredded with a fork.
   - Once cooked, shred the beef with two forks and mix it into the sauce. Keep warm.

2. Cook the rice:
   - Rinse the rice under cold water until the water runs clear.
   - In a medium pot, combine rice, water, and a pinch of salt. Bring to a boil, then reduce the heat to low, cover, and simmer for 15 minutes or until the rice is cooked and water is absorbed. Fluff with a fork and set aside.

3. Fry the plantains:
   - Heat olive oil in a skillet over medium heat.
   - Add the plantain slices and fry until golden brown, about 2-3 minutes per side.
   - Remove from the skillet and drain on a paper towel. Sprinkle with salt to taste.

4. Assemble the bowl:
   - In a serving bowl, add a generous portion of rice.
   - Top with the shredded beef mixture.
   - Arrange the fried plantains around the bowl.
   - Garnish with fresh parsley or cilantro and serve immediately.

Nutritional Info (Per Serving):
Calories: 650 kcal per serving
Fats: 32 g (10 g saturated)
Carbohydrates: 60 g (6 g fiber, 14 g sugar)
Protein: 35 g

Key nutrients: Iron, potassium (from plantains), magnesium, and zinc

Tips: Add a side of fresh cucumber salad to lighten the dish.

10. Grilled Salmon with Asparagus and Roasted Sweet Potatoes

Salmon is rich in iodine and omega-3 fatty acids, while sweet potatoes offer vitamin A, crucial for thyroid hormone synthesis.

Prep time: 10 minutes
Cooking time: 30 minutes
Servings: 2

Ingredients:
- **For the salmon**:
  - 2 salmon fillets (about 150g each)
  - 1 tablespoon olive oil
  - 1 lemon, sliced (for garnish)
  - Salt and pepper to taste
- **For the sweet potatoes**:
  - 1 large sweet potato, peeled and cubed
  - 1 tablespoon olive oil
  - 1 teaspoon paprika
  - Salt and pepper to taste
- **For the asparagus**:
  - 12-15 asparagus spears, trimmed
  - 1 tablespoon olive oil
  - Salt and pepper to taste
- Fresh parsley, chopped (for garnish)

Instructions:

1. Roast the sweet potatoes:
   - Preheat the oven to 400°F (200°C).
   - Toss the sweet potato cubes with olive oil, paprika, salt, and pepper.
   - Spread them on a baking sheet in a single layer and roast for 20-25 minutes, or until golden and crispy, flipping halfway through.

2. Grill the asparagus:
   - While the potatoes roast, heat 1 tablespoon of olive oil in a grill pan or skillet over medium heat.
   - Add the asparagus spears, season with salt and pepper, and grill for 5-7 minutes, turning occasionally, until tender and slightly charred. Set aside.

3. Grill the salmon:
   - Brush the salmon fillets with olive oil and season with salt and pepper.
   - Heat the grill pan (or outdoor grill) to medium-high heat.
   - Grill the salmon for 4-5 minutes per side, depending on thickness, until the fish is cooked through and has nice grill marks.
   - Remove from heat and top each fillet with a lemon slice.

4. Assemble the dish:
   - Arrange the grilled salmon on plates alongside the roasted sweet potatoes and grilled asparagus.
   - Garnish with freshly chopped parsley for a burst of color and added flavor.

Nutritional Info (Per Serving):
Calories: 500 kcal per serving
Fats: 28 g (6 g saturated)
Carbohydrates: 34 g (7 g fiber, 10 g sugar)
Protein: 35 g

Key nutrients: Omega-3 fatty acids, iodine, vitamin A (from sweet potatoes), and selenium

Tips: Sprinkle sesame seeds on the asparagus for added flavor.

11. Grilled Shrimp Salad with Cherry Tomatoes and Bell Peppers

This grilled shrimp salad is rich in selenium from the shrimp, while the fresh vegetables provide antioxidants that help reduce inflammation.

Prep time: 15 minutes
Cooking time: 10 minutes
Servings: 4

Ingredients:

- 1 lb (450 g) shrimp, peeled and deveined

- 1 cup cherry tomatoes, halved

- 1 yellow bell pepper, diced

- 1 red bell pepper, diced

- 2 tbsp extra-virgin olive oil

- 2 cloves garlic, minced

- Juice of 1 lemon

- Salt and black pepper to taste

- Fresh parsley, chopped (for garnish)

Instructions:

1. In a bowl, toss the shrimp with olive oil, minced garlic, lemon juice, salt, and pepper. Let marinate for 10-15 minutes.

2. Heat a grill pan or skillet over medium-high heat. Grill the shrimp for about 2-3 minutes on each side until they are pink and opaque.

3. In a large serving bowl, combine cherry tomatoes and diced bell peppers.

4. Add the grilled shrimp to the bowl, mixing gently.

5. Drizzle with a bit of extra olive oil, sprinkle with freshly chopped parsley, and adjust seasoning if needed.

6. Serve immediately, enjoying this light and refreshing salad as a perfect summer appetizer.

Nutritional Info (Per Serving):
Calories: 180 kcal per serving
Fats: 10 g (2 g saturated)
Carbohydrates: 6 g (2 g fiber, 3 g sugar)
Protein: 20 g

Key nutrients: Selenium, vitamin C (from bell peppers), magnesium

Tips: For an extra burst of flavor, add a drizzle of balsamic glaze.

12. Fresh Tuna Salad with Avocado, Cherry Tomatoes

Tuna is rich in iodine and omega-3 fatty acids, essential for thyroid health, while avocado adds magnesium and healthy fats.

Prep time: 10 minutes
Cooking time: None
Servings: 2

Ingredients:
- 200g fresh tuna, sliced into sashimi-style pieces
- 1 avocado, sliced
- 1 cup cherry tomatoes, halved
- 2 cups mixed greens (lettuce, spinach, or arugula)
- 1 tablespoon sesame seeds (white and black, mixed)
- 1 tablespoon tamari sauce (gluten-free)
- 1 tablespoon rice vinegar
- 1 tablespoon lemon juice
- Salt and pepper to taste

Instructions:

1. Prepare the dressing:
   - In a small bowl, whisk together the tamari sauce, rice vinegar, lemon juice, salt, and pepper. Set aside.

2. Assemble the salad:
   - In a large serving bowl, layer the mixed greens as the base.
   - Arrange the sliced tuna, avocado, and cherry tomatoes on top of the greens.

3. Dress and garnish:
   - Drizzle the prepared dressing over the salad.
   - Sprinkle with sesame seeds for added texture and flavor.

4. Serve:
   - Serve immediately as a light, fresh meal.

Nutritional Info (Per Serving):
Calories: 420 kcal per serving
Fats: 26 g (4 g saturated)
Carbohydrates: 12 g (4 g fiber, 5 g sugar)
Protein: 36 g

Key nutrients: Omega-3 fatty acids, iodine, magnesium, vitamin E

Tips: Serve with gluten-free crackers or a side of quinoa for a more filling meal.

13. Quinoa Chickpea Salad Bowl with Cucumber and Tomatoes

Quinoa and chickpeas are rich in plant-based protein and zinc, supporting healthy thyroid function and metabolism.

Prep time: 10 minutes
Cooking time: 5 minutes (if using pre-cooked quinoa)
Servings: 2

Ingredients:
- ½ cup cooked quinoa
- ½ cup cooked chickpeas (or canned, drained)
- 1 teaspoon paprika
- 1 tablespoon olive oil (for sautéing)
- ½ cup cherry tomatoes, halved
- ½ cucumber, sliced
- Fresh parsley, chopped (for garnish)
- 1 tablespoon lemon juice
- 1 tablespoon extra virgin olive oil (for dressing)
- Salt and pepper to taste

Instructions:
1. Cook the chickpeas:
   - If using canned chickpeas, drain and rinse them.
   - Heat olive oil in a skillet over medium heat. Add the chickpeas and paprika, and sauté for 5-7 minutes until they are slightly crispy and coated with the spices. Remove from heat.

2. Prepare the quinoa:
   - If you haven't already, cook the quinoa according to package instructions. Set aside and let it cool slightly.

3. Assemble the salad:
   - In a bowl, layer the cooked quinoa, spiced chickpeas, halved cherry tomatoes, and cucumber slices.

4. Dress the salad:
   - In a small bowl, whisk together lemon juice, extra virgin olive oil, salt, and pepper. Drizzle the dressing over the salad.

5. Garnish:

- Sprinkle fresh parsley on top for an extra burst of flavor. Serve immediately.

Nutritional Info (Per Serving):
Calories: 420 kcal per serving
Fats: 18 g (2.5 g saturated)
Carbohydrates: 50 g (7 g fiber, 5 g sugar)
Protein: 14 g

Key nutrients: Zinc, folate, magnesium, iron

Tips: Add a sprinkle of za'atar spice for added flavor.

14. Beef Pho (Vietnamese Noodle Soup)

This traditional Vietnamese noodle soup is rich in flavor, featuring beef broth, tender beef slices, rice noodles, and fresh herbs like basil and mint. The beef provides zinc and iron, while the herbs and spices help reduce inflammation and support overall thyroid health.

Prep time: 15 minutes
Cooking time: 45 minutes
Servings: 4

Ingredients:
- **For the broth:**
  - 1 liter beef broth (preferably homemade or low-sodium)
  - 1 onion, halved
  - 2-inch piece of fresh ginger, sliced
  - 2 cinnamon sticks
  - 3 whole star anise
  - 4 whole cloves
  - 1 tablespoon fish sauce
  - 1 tablespoon soy-free tamari (optional)
  - Salt to taste
- **For the beef:**
  - 200g beef sirloin or brisket, thinly sliced
- **For the noodles:**
  - 200g rice noodles (pho noodles)
- **Toppings:**
  - Fresh Thai basil
  - Fresh mint leaves
  - Bean sprouts
  - 1 red chili, sliced
  - Lime wedges
  - Green onions, chopped
  - Hoisin sauce and sriracha (optional for serving)

Instructions:

1. Prepare the broth:
   - In a large pot, bring the beef broth to a boil.
   - Add the onion, ginger, cinnamon sticks, star anise, and cloves.
   - Reduce the heat and let the broth simmer for 30-40 minutes to allow the spices to infuse the liquid.

- Add fish sauce and tamari for extra umami flavor. Season with salt to taste. Strain the broth to remove the solids and return the clear broth to the pot.

2. Prepare the noodles:
   - While the broth is simmering, cook the rice noodles according to the package instructions. Drain and set aside.

3. Prepare the beef:
   - Thinly slice the beef sirloin or brisket. Set aside.
   - If using brisket, you can cook it briefly in the broth until tender, then slice it.

4. Assemble the pho:
   - Divide the cooked rice noodles into individual bowls.
   - Arrange the thinly sliced beef over the noodles.
   - Ladle the hot broth over the beef and noodles. The hot broth will cook the beef slices instantly.

5. Garnish and serve:
   - Garnish each bowl with fresh basil, mint leaves, bean sprouts, sliced chili, and green onions.
   - Serve with lime wedges on the side and offer hoisin sauce or sriracha for extra flavor if desired.

Nutritional Info (Per Serving):
Calories: 450 kcal per serving
Fats: 12 g (3 g saturated)
Carbohydrates: 50 g (4 g fiber, 3 g sugar)
Protein: 28 g

Key nutrients: Zinc, iron, vitamin C (from herbs), and manganese

Tips: Adjust the spice level by adding more chili slices or a drizzle of sriracha.

15. Fish Stew with Vegetables

This stew is packed with fresh vegetables, tender pieces of fish, and herbs in a light tomato-based broth. Fish is an excellent source of iodine and selenium, crucial for thyroid function, while the vegetables provide a rich mix of vitamins and minerals.

Prep time: 15 minutes
Cooking time: 35 minutes
Servings: 4

Ingredients:
- **For the stew:**
  - 500g white fish fillets (such as cod or halibut), cut into chunks
  - 1 tablespoon olive oil
  - 1 onion, chopped
  - 2 garlic cloves, minced
  - 1 bell pepper, diced
  - 2 carrots, sliced
  - 2 medium potatoes, peeled and cubed
  - 1 can (400g) diced tomatoes
  - 4 cups fish or vegetable broth
  - 1 teaspoon smoked paprika
  - 1 teaspoon dried thyme
  - Salt and pepper to taste
- **For garnish:**
  - Fresh parsley, chopped
  - Lemon wedges (optional)

Instructions:

1. Sauté the vegetables:
   - Heat the olive oil in a large pot over medium heat.
   - Add the chopped onion and garlic, and sauté for 3-4 minutes until softened and fragrant.
   - Add the diced bell pepper, sliced carrots, and cubed potatoes, and cook for another 5 minutes, stirring occasionally.

2. Add the broth and seasonings:
   - Stir in the diced tomatoes, smoked paprika, thyme, and broth.
   - Season with salt and pepper to taste.
   - Bring the mixture to a boil, then reduce the heat to low. Cover and simmer for 20-25 minutes, or until the potatoes and carrots are tender.

3. Cook the fish:
   - Gently add the fish chunks to the pot and simmer for an additional 5-7 minutes, or until the fish is cooked through and flakes easily with a fork. Be careful not to overcook the fish.

4. Serve and garnish:
   - Ladle the stew into bowls.
   - Garnish with freshly chopped parsley and serve with lemon wedges on the side for a bright, citrusy touch.

Nutritional Info (Per Serving):
Calories: 380 kcal per serving
Fats: 12 g (2 g saturated)
Carbohydrates: 40 g (5 g fiber, 6 g sugar)
Protein: 28 g

Key nutrients: Iodine, selenium, vitamin A, potassium

Tips: Add a splash of white wine during cooking for extra depth of flavor.

16. Grilled Honey Garlic Salmon with Brown Rice

This delicious grilled salmon is glazed with a honey garlic sauce and served over a bed of warm brown rice. Salmon is a great source of omega-3 fatty acids and selenium, both of which help maintain thyroid health, while brown rice provides steady energy.

Prep time: 15 minutes
Cooking time: 35 minutes
Servings: 2

Ingredients:
- **For the salmon:**
  - 2 salmon fillets
  - 2 tablespoons honey
  - 1 tablespoon coconut aminos (or soy-free tamari for thyroid-friendly)
  - 1 tablespoon olive oil
  - 2 cloves garlic, minced
  - 1 tablespoon lemon juice
  - Salt and pepper to taste
- **For the rice:**
  - 1 cup brown rice
  - 2 cups water
  - Salt to taste
- **For garnish:**
  - Fresh parsley, chopped
  - Lemon wedges

Instructions:

1. Cook the brown rice:
   - Rinse the brown rice under cold water.
   - In a medium saucepan, combine the rice, water and a pinch of salt. Bring to a boil, then reduce the heat to low, cover, and simmer for 30-35 minutes, or until the rice is cooked and the water is absorbed. Fluff with a fork and set aside.

2. Prepare the honey garlic glaze:
   - In a small bowl, whisk together the honey, coconut aminos, olive oil, minced garlic, and lemon juice.
   - Season the salmon fillets with salt and pepper, then brush the glaze over the fillets.

3. Grill the salmon:
   - Preheat a grill or grill pan to medium-high heat.

- Place the salmon fillets on the grill, skin side down, and cook for 4-5 minutes on each side, brushing with more glaze as they cook. The salmon should be cooked through and slightly caramelized on top.

4. Assemble the dish:
   - Divide the cooked brown rice between plates.
   - Place the grilled salmon on top of the rice and drizzle with any remaining glaze.
   - Garnish with freshly chopped parsley and serve with lemon wedges for extra brightness.

Nutritional Info (Per Serving):
Calories: 520 kcal per serving
Fats: 18 g (4 g saturated)
Carbohydrates: 50 g (4 g fiber, 8 g sugar)
Protein: 35 g

Key nutrients: Omega-3 fatty acids, selenium, vitamin B12, magnesium

Tips: For a crispy salmon skin, grill skin-side down first, and avoid flipping too often.

17. Chicken Fried Rice with Vegetables and a Fried Egg

This easy and delicious chicken fried rice is packed with veggies, tender chicken, and topped with a sunny-side-up egg for added protein and flavor. The chicken and eggs provide selenium and iodine, and the vegetables are packed with antioxidants to support overall thyroid health.

Prep time: 15 minutes
Cooking time: 15 minutes
Servings: 4

Ingredients:
- **For the fried rice:**
  - 2 cups cooked white rice (preferably day-old)
  - 200g cooked chicken breast, shredded or chopped
  - 1 tablespoon coconut aminos (or soy-free tamari for thyroid-friendly)
  - 2 tablespoons olive oil (divided)
  - 1 small onion, chopped
  - 1 cup frozen mixed vegetables (peas, carrots, corn)
  - 1 bell pepper, diced
  - 2 green onions, chopped
  - 1 clove garlic, minced
  - 2 eggs, beaten (for the fried rice)
- **For the fried egg topping:**
  - 1 egg (per serving)
  - 1 teaspoon olive oil (for frying)
- **Garnish:**
  - Sesame seeds
  - Fresh cilantro or parsley (optional)

Instructions:

1. Cook the vegetables and chicken:
   - Heat 1 tablespoon of olive oil in a large skillet or wok over medium heat.
   - Add the chopped onion, diced bell pepper, and minced garlic. Sauté for 2-3 minutes until fragrant.
   - Add the mixed vegetables and cook for another 3-4 minutes until they are tender.
   - Stir in the cooked chicken and cook for 2 minutes until heated through. Remove from the skillet and set aside.

2. Scramble the eggs:

- In the same skillet, add the beaten eggs and scramble them until fully cooked. Set the scrambled eggs aside with the chicken and vegetables.

3. Fry the rice:
   - Add the remaining tablespoon of olive oil to the skillet, then add the cooked rice. Break up any clumps and stir-fry for 3-4 minutes until the rice is heated through and slightly crispy.
   - Add the coconut aminos (or tamari) and mix well. Return the chicken, vegetables, and scrambled eggs to the skillet, and toss everything together.

4. Fry the egg topping:
   - In a small pan, heat 1 teaspoon of olive oil over medium heat.
   - Crack the egg into the pan and fry until the whites are set but the yolk remains runny, about 2-3 minutes.

5. Assemble the dish:
   - Serve the fried rice in individual bowls.
   - Top each serving with a fried egg.
   - Garnish with sesame seeds and fresh cilantro or parsley if desired.

Nutritional Info (Per Serving):
Calories: 550 kcal per serving
Fats: 22 g (5 g saturated)
Carbohydrates: 60 g (5 g fiber, 6 g sugar)
Protein: 28 g

Key nutrients: Selenium, vitamin C, choline, potassium

Tips: Use day-old rice for the best texture, as freshly cooked rice can become mushy during stir-frying.

18. Mediterranean Grilled Chicken Salad

This Mediterranean Salad has high-quality protein, healthy fats, and nutrient-rich ingredients like eggs and leafy greens, which provide selenium, iodine, and essential vitamins.

Prep time: 10 minutes
Cooking time: 15 minutes
Servings: 2

Ingredients:
- 1 grilled chicken breast, sliced
- 2 cups mixed salad greens (aragula, spinach, romaine)
- 2 hard-boiled eggs, sliced
- ½ cup cherry tomatoes, halved
- ¼ cup mixed olives (Kalamata, green olives)
- ¼ cup white beans (canned, drained, and rinsed)
- 1 tbsp extra virgin olive oil
- 1 tbsp balsamic vinegar
- Salt and black pepper to taste

Instructions:

1. In a large bowl, place the mixed salad greens as the base.
2. Add the halved cherry tomatoes, olives, white beans, and sliced eggs on top of the greens.
3. Arrange the grilled chicken slices neatly on top.
4. Drizzle with olive oil and balsamic vinegar, and season with salt and pepper.
5. Toss gently before serving and enjoy this fresh, protein-packed salad.

Nutritional Info (Per Serving):
Calories: 320 kcal per serving
Fats: 18 g (3 g saturated)
Carbohydrates: 12 g (4 g fiber, 6 g sugar)
Protein: 28 g

Key nutrients: Selenium, iodine, vitamin E, vitamin K

Tips: Add a handful of toasted pine nuts for added flavor and texture.

19. Garlic Shrimp with Zucchini Noodles, Cherry Tomatoes, and Olives

This vibrant is a quick, low-carb meal full of Mediterranean flavors. Shrimp is high in selenium, essential for thyroid hormone metabolism, while zucchini provides antioxidants to support overall health.

Prep time: 15 minutes
Cooking time: 10 minutes
Servings: 2

Ingredients:
- **For the shrimp**:
  - 300g shrimp, peeled and deveined
  - 1 tablespoon olive oil
  - 2 cloves garlic, minced
  - 1 teaspoon paprika
  - Salt and pepper to taste
- **For the zucchini noodles**:
  - 2 medium zucchinis, spiralized
  - 1 tablespoon olive oil
  - Salt and pepper to taste
- **For the toppings**:
  - 1 cup cherry tomatoes, halved
  - ¼ cup black or Kalamata olives, pitted
  - 2 tablespoons fresh parsley, chopped (for garnish)
  - 1 tablespoon lemon juice (optional)

Instructions:

1. Cook the shrimp:
   - Heat 1 tablespoon of olive oil in a large skillet over medium heat.
   - Add minced garlic and sauté for 1 minute until fragrant.
   - Add the shrimp, paprika, salt, and pepper. Cook for 3-4 minutes on each side, or until the shrimp turn pink and are fully cooked. Remove from heat and set aside.

2. Prepare the zucchini noodles:
   - In the same skillet, add another tablespoon of olive oil over medium heat.
   - Add the spiralized zucchini noodles (zoodles), season with salt and pepper, and cook for 2-3 minutes, tossing gently. The zoodles should be tender but still slightly crisp. Remove from heat.

3. Assemble the dish:
   - In a serving bowl, arrange the cooked zoodles.
   - Top with the cooked shrimp, halved cherry tomatoes, and black olives.
   - Garnish with freshly chopped parsley and a squeeze of lemon juice, if desired, for added brightness.

Nutritional Info (Per Serving):
Calories: 350 kcal per serving
Fats: 22 g (3.5 g saturated)
Carbohydrates: 12 g (3 g fiber, 5 g sugar)
Protein: 28 g

Key nutrients: Selenium, vitamin C, potassium, magnesium

Tips: Use a spiralizer for perfectly shaped zucchini noodles and avoid overcooking to maintain their crisp texture.

20. Thyroid-Friendly Bibimbap (Korean Rice Bowl)

This vibrant and healthy Bibimbap bowl is made without soy and features fresh vegetables, marinated beef (with coconut aminos), and rice, topped with sesame seeds and a spicy gochujang sauce. The combination of coconut aminos, fresh vegetables, and protein-rich beef ensures you get iodine, zinc, and essential amino acids for optimal thyroid function.

Prep time: 20 minutes
Cooking time: 25 minutes
Servings: 4

Ingredients:
- **For the beef:**
  - 200g ground beef or sliced beef (sirloin or ribeye)
  - 2 tablespoons coconut aminos
  - 1 tablespoon olive oil
  - 1 tablespoon honey or sugar
  - 2 cloves garlic, minced
  - 1 teaspoon ground ginger
  - 1 tablespoon sesame seeds
- **For the vegetables:**
  - 1 cup carrots, julienned
  - 1 cup bean sprouts
  - 1 cup cucumbers, sliced
  - 1 cup mushrooms, sliced (shiitake or button mushrooms)
  - 1 tablespoon olive oil
- **For the rice:**
  - 2 cups cooked white rice
- **For the sauce:**
  - 2 tablespoons gochujang (Korean chili paste)
  - 1 tablespoon olive oil
  - 1 tablespoon rice vinegar
  - 1 tablespoon honey
- **Toppings**:
  - 1 fresh red chili, sliced (optional for garnish)
  - Sesame seeds for garnish
  - Sliced green onions (optional)

Instructions:

1. Marinate and cook the beef:

- In a bowl, combine coconut aminos, olive oil, honey, minced garlic, ground ginger, and sesame seeds.
- Add the beef and marinate for 15-20 minutes.
- Heat a skillet over medium-high heat and cook the marinated beef for 5-7 minutes until browned and fully cooked. Set aside.

2. Cook the vegetables:
   - In a separate skillet, heat 1 tablespoon of olive oil and sauté the mushrooms for about 5 minutes until softened. Set aside.
   - Sauté the bean sprouts in the same pan for 2-3 minutes and set aside.
   - Lightly sauté the julienned carrots in olive oil for 2 minutes until just tender. Remove from heat.

3. Prepare the rice:
   - Cook the white rice according to package instructions, then fluff it and keep it warm.

4. Make the gochujang sauce:
   - In a small bowl, mix together gochujang, olive oil, rice vinegar, and honey. Adjust to taste by adding more honey for sweetness or more gochujang for spice.

5. Assemble the Bibimbap:
   - In individual bowls, place a portion of the cooked rice at the bottom.
   - Arrange the cooked vegetables (carrots, bean sprouts, cucumbers, and mushrooms) around the rice.
   - Add the cooked beef to the center of the bowl.
   - Drizzle with the gochujang sauce.
   - Garnish with sliced red chili, sesame seeds, and green onions if desired.

Nutritional Info (Per Serving):
Calories: 490 kcal per serving
Fats: 20 g (4 g saturated)
Carbohydrates: 55 g (5 g fiber, 8 g sugar)
Protein: 24 g

Key nutrients: Zinc, iodine, vitamin A, manganese

Tips: Adjust the spice level of the gochujang sauce based on your heat preference.

Chapter 7: Dinner Recipes

Dinner is more than just a meal—it's a time to slow down, connect, and nourish your body after a long day. It's the perfect opportunity to recharge and unwind with wholesome, flavorful dishes that satisfy both your taste buds and your health goals. In this collection of 25 dinner recipes, we've brought together an exciting variety of proteins, grains, and vibrant vegetables to create meals that are not only delicious but also packed with essential nutrients to support your overall well-being.

Whether you're in the mood for hearty beef and lamb dishes, comforting chicken recipes, or light and fresh seafood options, these dinners have something for everyone. Each recipe is thoughtfully crafted to deliver a balance of textures and flavors, from the tenderness of slow-cooked meats to the crunch of roasted vegetables. With ingredients chosen for their health benefits, you can feel confident knowing that these meals are not only tasty but also nourishing, helping you feel your best.

From globally inspired flavors to cozy classics, this collection ensures that dinner becomes a highlight of your day. Whether you're gathering around the table with family or enjoying a quiet evening to yourself, these recipes provide the perfect balance of indulgence and nourishment. Dive into a world of delicious possibilities and discover how satisfying a healthy, home-cooked dinner can be!

1. Grilled Chicken with Quinoa and Roasted Vegetables

This dish combines lean protein and antioxidant-rich vegetables with quinoa, which is high in magnesium, selenium, and zinc to support thyroid health.

Prep Time: 15 minutes
Cooking Time: 40 minutes
Servings: 2

Ingredients:
- **For the chicken:**
  - 2 chicken breasts
  - 1 tablespoon olive oil
  - 1 teaspoon garlic powder
  - 1 teaspoon smoked paprika
  - Salt and pepper to taste

- **For the quinoa:**
  - 1 cup quinoa
  - 2 cups water or broth
  - Salt to taste

- **For the roasted vegetables:**
  - 1 zucchini, sliced
  - 1 red bell pepper, sliced
  - 1 yellow bell pepper, sliced
  - 1 cup cherry tomatoes
  - 1 large carrot, sliced
  - 1 cup broccoli florets
  - 1 tablespoon olive oil
  - Salt and pepper to taste
  - Fresh parsley for garnish

Instructions:

1. Prepare the quinoa:
   - Rinse the quinoa under cold water, then add it to a pot with water or broth and a pinch of salt.
   - Bring to a boil, then reduce to a simmer and cook for about 15 minutes, or until the quinoa is fluffy and all the liquid is absorbed.

2. Marinate and grill the chicken:
   - Rub the chicken breasts with olive oil, garlic powder, smoked paprika, salt, and pepper.
   - Preheat a grill or grill pan over medium-high heat.
   - Grill the chicken for 5-7 minutes per side, or until fully cooked through. Let the chicken rest for 5 minutes before slicing.

3. Roast the vegetables:
   - Preheat the oven to 400°F (200°C).
   - Toss the zucchini, bell peppers, cherry tomatoes, carrots, and broccoli with olive oil, salt, and pepper.
   - Spread the vegetables evenly on a baking sheet and roast for 15-20 minutes, or until tender and slightly caramelized.

4. Assemble the plate:
   - Serve the grilled chicken over a bed of cooked quinoa.
   - Arrange the roasted vegetables around the chicken.
   - Garnish with fresh parsley and a drizzle of olive oil if desired.

Nutritional Info (Per Serving):
Calories: 480 kcal per serving
Fats: 18 g (3 g saturated)
Carbohydrates: 45 g (7 g fiber, 8 g sugar)
Protein: 40 g

Key Nutrients: Protein, magnesium, selenium, zinc, vitamin C, and fiber

Tips: Marinate the chicken for an extra 15 minutes for more depth of flavor.

2. Grilled Salmon with Butternut Squash Purée

This dish is nutrient-dense and rich in omega-3 fatty acids from the salmon, the butternut squash provides vitamin A and antioxidants, making it a wholesome and flavorful meal.

Prep Time: 15 minutes
Cooking Time: 30 minutes
Servings: 2

Ingredients:
- 2 salmon fillets (about 6 oz each)
- 1 tablespoon olive oil
- Salt and pepper, to taste
- 1 small butternut squash, peeled and cubed
- 1 tablespoon unsalted butter
- 1/4 cup chicken or vegetable broth
- 1 teaspoon fresh thyme leaves
- Microgreens, for garnish (optional)
- Lemon slices, for garnish

Instructions:

1. Prepare the Butternut Squash Purée: In a medium saucepan, boil the butternut squash cubes in salted water for about 15-20 minutes, or until tender. Drain and place the squash in a blender. Add butter, chicken broth, thyme, and blend until smooth. Season with salt and pepper. Set aside.

2. Grill the Salmon: While the squash is cooking, heat a grill pan or outdoor grill over medium-high heat. Rub the salmon fillets with olive oil, salt, and pepper. Grill the salmon skin-side down for about 3-4 minutes per side, or until the salmon is just cooked through and flakes easily with a fork.

3. Serve: On each plate, spread a generous amount of the butternut squash purée. Place the grilled salmon on top. Garnish with fresh microgreens and a lemon slice. Enjoy!

Nutritional Info (Per Serving):
Calories: 520 kcal per serving
Fats: 32 g (6 g saturated)
Carbohydrates: 20 g (3 g fiber, 6 g sugar)
Protein: 35 g

Key Nutrients: Omega-3s, vitamin A, selenium, and magnesium

Tips: For a creamier purée, add a splash of coconut milk instead of broth. Garnish with toasted pumpkin seeds for an extra crunch.

3. Grilled Lamb Chops with Rosemary Sweet Potato Fries

This dish is rich in protein, zinc, iron, and essential vitamins, supporting muscle repair and energy metabolism. The sweet potatoes provide fiber and antioxidants, while olive oil and rosemary offer heart-healthy fats and anti-inflammatory benefits, making this a well-rounded and nutritious meal.

Prep Time: 30 minutes (including marinating)
Cooking Time: 30 minutes
Servings: 2

Ingredients:
- **For the lamb chops:**
  - 4 lamb chops
  - 2 tablespoons olive oil
  - 2 cloves garlic, minced
  - 1 tablespoon fresh rosemary, chopped
  - Salt and pepper to taste

- **For the sweet potato fries:**
  - 2 large sweet potatoes, peeled and cut into fries
  - 2 tablespoons olive oil
  - 1 teaspoon dried rosemary (or fresh)
  - Salt and pepper to taste

- **For garnish:**
  - Fresh rosemary sprigs

Instructions:

1. Prepare the lamb chops:
   - In a small bowl, mix the olive oil, minced garlic, chopped rosemary, salt, and pepper.
   - Rub the lamb chops with the mixture and let them marinate for at least 30 minutes (the longer, the better for flavor).

2. Grill the lamb chops:
   - Preheat the grill to medium-high heat.
   - Grill the lamb chops for about 4-5 minutes per side for medium-rare (adjust the time to your preferred level of doneness).
   - Once done, remove from the grill and let them rest for a few minutes.

3. Prepare the sweet potato fries:
   - Preheat the oven to 425°F (220°C).
   - Toss the sweet potato fries with olive oil, rosemary, salt, and pepper.
   - Spread the fries on a baking sheet in a single layer.
   - Roast for 25-30 minutes, flipping halfway through, until they are golden and crispy.

4. Assemble the dish:
   - Serve the grilled lamb chops alongside the crispy rosemary sweet potato fries.
   - Garnish with fresh rosemary sprigs for an aromatic touch.
   - Optionally, you can drizzle a little more olive oil or serve with your favorite dipping sauce.

Nutritional Info (Per Serving):
Calories: 600 kcal per serving
Fats: 35 g (9 g saturated)
Carbohydrates: 45 g (6 g fiber, 10 g sugar)
Protein: 35 g

Key Nutrients: Protein, iron, zinc, fiber, and vitamin A

Tips: Marinate the lamb overnight for maximum flavor. Serve with a side of mint yogurt sauce for a fresh twist.

4. Grilled Filet Mignon with Garlic Mashed Potatoes

This meal is rich in high-quality protein from the steak and provides a good source of potassium and vitamin C from the potatoes. The garlic in the mashed potatoes adds anti-inflammatory benefits.

Prep Time: 15 minutes
Cooking Time: 25 minutes
Servings: 2

Ingredients:
- 2 filet mignon steaks (6 oz each)
- 1 tablespoon olive oil
- Salt and pepper, to taste
- 1 sprig of fresh rosemary (for garnish)

For the Garlic Mashed Potatoes:
- 4 medium russet potatoes, peeled and cubed
- 3 tablespoons unsalted butter
- 1/4 cup heavy cream (or milk for a lighter option)
- 2 cloves garlic, minced
- Salt and pepper, to taste
- Fresh chives or rosemary (optional, for garnish)

Instructions:

1. Prepare the Garlic Mashed Potatoes:
   - In a large pot, boil the cubed potatoes in salted water for about 15 minutes or until tender. Drain the water.
   - Mash the potatoes with butter, heavy cream, and minced garlic. Season with salt and pepper to taste. Keep warm.

2. Grill the Filet Mignon:
   - Preheat your grill or grill pan to medium-high heat. Rub the filet mignon steaks with olive oil, and season with salt and pepper on both sides.
   - Grill the steaks for about 4-5 minutes per side for medium-rare, or adjust the time for your desired doneness.
   - Remove the steaks from the grill and let them rest for 5 minutes.

3. Serve:

- Plate the grilled filet mignon alongside a generous serving of garlic mashed potatoes. Garnish the steak with a sprig of rosemary and sprinkle fresh herbs (chives or rosemary) over the potatoes if desired. Serve hot and enjoy!

Nutritional Info (Per Serving):
Calories: 540 kcal per serving
Fats: 27 g (9 g saturated)
Carbohydrates: 35 g (4 g fiber, 2 g sugar)
Protein: 42 g

Key Nutrients: Protein, potassium, vitamin C, and selenium

Tips: Let the filet mignon rest for at least 5 minutes before serving to lock in the juices. Add roasted garlic to the mashed potatoes for an extra depth of flavor.

5. Stuffed Bell Peppers

These stuffed bell peppers are packed with lean protein from the ground beef, while quinoa adds fiber and essential amino acids for digestion and overall wellness. The bell peppers are rich in vitamin C and antioxidants, boosting immune health and reducing inflammation.

Prep Time: 15 minutes
Cooking Time: 35 minutes
Servings: 6

Ingredients:
- 6 large bell peppers (any color)
- 500g ground beef
- 1 cup cooked quinoa
- 1 medium onion, finely chopped
- 3 cloves garlic, minced
- 1 can (400g) diced tomatoes, drained
- 1 tsp dried oregano
- 1 tsp paprika
- 1/2 tsp ground cumin
- Salt and pepper to taste
- 1/2 cup shredded mozzarella or parmesan cheese (optional)
- Olive oil for sautéing

Instructions:

1. Prepare the Peppers: Preheat your oven to 375°F (190°C). Slice off the tops of the bell peppers and remove the seeds and membranes. Lightly coat the peppers with olive oil and place them in a baking dish. Roast the peppers in the oven for 10 minutes to soften slightly.

2. Cook the Filling: Heat a tablespoon of olive oil in a large pan over medium heat. Add the chopped onions and garlic, cooking until softened and fragrant, about 3-4 minutes. Add the ground beef and cook until browned, breaking it up with a spoon.

3. Mix in the Ingredients: Stir in the cooked quinoa, diced tomatoes, oregano, paprika, cumin, salt, and pepper. Let the mixture simmer for another 5 minutes, allowing the flavors to meld together.

4. Stuff the Peppers: Remove the bell peppers from the oven. Generously fill each pepper with the beef and quinoa mixture. If using cheese, sprinkle the shredded cheese on top of each stuffed pepper.

5. Bake: Place the stuffed peppers back into the oven and bake for 20-25 minutes, or until the peppers are tender and the filling is heated through. If you added cheese, you want it to be melted and bubbly.

6. Serve: Remove the stuffed peppers from the oven and let them cool for a few minutes before serving. These peppers are hearty enough to serve as a complete meal.

Nutritional Info (Per Serving):
Calories: 350 kcal per serving
Fats: 18 g (7 g saturated)
Carbohydrates: 26 g (6 g fiber, 10 g sugar)
Protein: 22 g

Key Nutrients: Protein, fiber, vitamin C, and selenium

Tips: Use a variety of colored bell peppers for a visually stunning presentation. Add some red pepper flakes for a slight kick.

6. Grilled Steak with Rosemary, Asparagus, and Roasted Potatoes

Steak offers iron and zinc for thyroid hormone production, while asparagus provides folate and vitamin K for overall health.

Prep Time: 20 minutes
Cooking Time: 30 minutes
Servings: 2

Ingredients:
- **For the steak:**
  - 2 ribeye steaks (or your preferred cut)
  - 1 tablespoon olive oil
  - 2 sprigs fresh rosemary
  - Salt and pepper to taste
  - 2 cloves garlic, minced

- **For the roasted potatoes:**
  - 2 large potatoes, cubed
  - 1 tablespoon olive oil
  - 1 teaspoon dried thyme
  - Salt and pepper to taste

- **For the asparagus:**
  - 1 bunch asparagus, trimmed
  - 1 tablespoon olive oil
  - Salt and pepper to taste

Instructions:

1. Prepare the potatoes:
   - Preheat the oven to 400°F (200°C).
   - Toss the cubed potatoes with olive oil, dried thyme, salt, and pepper.
   - Spread the potatoes in a single layer on a baking sheet and roast for 25-30 minutes, flipping halfway through, until golden and crispy.

2. Prepare the steak:

- While the potatoes are roasting, rub the steaks with olive oil, minced garlic, salt, and pepper. Place fresh rosemary sprigs on top of the steaks and let them rest for 10-15 minutes to absorb the flavors.
    - Heat a grill or grill pan over medium-high heat.
    - Grill the steaks for 4-5 minutes per side for medium-rare, or adjust to your preferred level of doneness.
    - Remove from the heat and let the steaks rest for 5 minutes before serving.

3. Cook the asparagus:
    - While the steak rests, toss the asparagus with olive oil, salt, and pepper.
    - Grill or roast the asparagus for 5-7 minutes, until tender but still slightly crisp.

4. Serve:
    - Plate the grilled steak alongside the roasted potatoes and grilled asparagus. Garnish with an additional rosemary sprig for an aromatic finish.

Nutritional Info (Per Serving):
Calories: 650 kcal per serving
Fats: 35 g (10 g saturated)
Carbohydrates: 45 g (5 g fiber, 6 g sugar)
Protein: 45 g

Key Nutrients: Protein, iron, zinc, vitamin K, and fiber

Tips: Use fresh thyme or oregano if rosemary isn't available. Add a squeeze of lemon juice to the asparagus for a zesty finish.

7. Grilled Salmon with Quinoa and Roasted Vegetables

This is a wholesome and balanced meal, offering lean protein, omega-3 fatty acids, and plenty of vitamins and minerals from the vegetables. The lemon and fresh herbs add a bright and refreshing flavor to the dish, making it perfect for a healthy and satisfying dinner.

Prep Time: 15 minutes
Cooking Time: 25 minutes
Servings: 2

Ingredients:
- **For the salmon:**
  - 2 salmon fillets
  - 1 tablespoon olive oil
  - 1 teaspoon lemon juice
  - Salt and pepper to taste
  - Fresh parsley for garnish
  - Lemon slices for serving

- **For the quinoa:**
  - 1 cup quinoa
  - 2 cups water or vegetable broth
  - Salt to taste

- **For the roasted vegetables:**
  - 1 large carrot, peeled and sliced
  - 1 cup broccoli florets
  - 1 tablespoon olive oil
  - Salt and pepper to taste

Instructions:

1. Prepare the quinoa:
   - Rinse the quinoa under cold water.
   - In a pot, bring the water or vegetable broth to a boil. Add the quinoa and a pinch of salt.
   - Lower the heat, cover, and simmer for about 15 minutes until the quinoa is fluffy and the liquid is absorbed.

2. Roast the vegetables:
   - Preheat the oven to 400°F (200°C).

- Toss the sliced carrots and broccoli florets with olive oil, salt, and pepper.
- Spread the vegetables evenly on a baking sheet and roast for 20-25 minutes, or until they are tender and slightly caramelized.

3. Grill the salmon:
   - Rub the salmon fillets with olive oil, lemon juice, salt, and pepper.
   - Preheat a grill or grill pan over medium heat.
   - Grill the salmon fillets for about 4-5 minutes per side, or until they are cooked through and have a nice char.

4. Assemble the plate:
   - Serve the grilled salmon over a bed of quinoa.
   - Arrange the roasted carrots and broccoli around the salmon.
   - Garnish with fresh parsley and lemon slices for an extra burst of freshness.

Nutritional Info (Per Serving):
Calories: 500 kcal per serving
Fats: 22 g (5 g saturated)
Carbohydrates: 40 g (6 g fiber, 4 g sugar)
Protein: 40 g

Key Nutrients: Omega-3s, selenium, fiber, magnesium, and vitamin C

Tips: Marinate the salmon in lemon juice and olive oil for at least 15 minutes before grilling to enhance the flavor. Use vegetable broth for the quinoa to add more depth to the dish.

8. Hearty Beef Stew with Root Vegetables

Packed with iron and zinc from beef and antioxidants from root vegetables, this stew promotes energy production and overall thyroid health.

Prep Time: 20 minutes
Cooking Time: 2 hours
Servings: 6

Ingredients:
- 2 pounds (900g) beef chuck, cut into bite-sized cubes
- 2 tablespoons olive oil
- 1 onion, diced
- 2 cloves garlic, minced
- 3 carrots, peeled and chopped
- 2 potatoes, peeled and cubed
- 1 parsnip, chopped
- 1 bell pepper, chopped
- 1 tablespoon tomato paste
- 1 teaspoon dried thyme
- 2 sprigs fresh rosemary
- 4 cups beef broth (or stock)
- 1 cup red wine (optional)
- Salt and pepper to taste
- 2 tablespoons fresh parsley, chopped (for garnish)

Instructions:

1. Sear the beef:
   - Heat 2 tablespoons of olive oil in a large pot or Dutch oven over medium-high heat.
   - Season the beef cubes with salt and pepper. Sear them in batches until browned on all sides (about 5 minutes per batch). Remove the beef and set it aside.

2. Cook the vegetables:
   - In the same pot, add the diced onion and garlic. Cook until softened, about 3 minutes.
   - Add the carrots, potatoes, parsnips, and bell pepper, cooking for another 5 minutes, stirring occasionally.

3. Add tomato paste and seasonings:
   - Stir in the tomato paste, thyme, and fresh rosemary sprigs. Let cook for 1-2 minutes to bring out the flavors.

4. Simmer the stew:
   - Add the seared beef back into the pot along with any juices. Pour in the beef broth and red wine (if using). Stir everything to combine.
   - Bring the stew to a simmer, cover the pot, and reduce the heat to low. Let it simmer for 1.5 to 2 hours, or until the beef is tender and the vegetables are cooked through. Stir occasionally.

5. Season and serve:
   - Taste the stew and adjust seasoning with salt and pepper as needed.
   - Garnish with freshly chopped parsley before serving.

Nutritional Info (Per Serving):
Calories: 450 kcal per serving
Fats: 25 g (8 g saturated)
Carbohydrates: 20 g (5 g fiber, 5 g sugar)
Protein: 35 g

Key Nutrients: Iron, zinc, potassium, vitamin C, and fiber

Tips: Let the stew simmer longer for even more tender beef and enhanced flavors. Serve with crusty gluten-free bread for a complete meal.

9. Grilled Chicken Fajitas with Bell Peppers and Onions

High in lean protein and packed with vitamin C from bell peppers, this dish supports metabolism and immune function.

Prep Time: 20 minutes
Cooking Time: 15 minutes
Servings: 4

Ingredients:
- **For the chicken:**
  - 2 chicken breasts, cut into strips
  - 1 tablespoon olive oil
  - 1 teaspoon cumin
  - 1 teaspoon chili powder
  - 1 teaspoon paprika
  - 1 teaspoon garlic powder
  - Salt and pepper to taste
  - Juice of 1 lime

- **For the vegetables:**
  - 1 red bell pepper, sliced
  - 1 yellow bell pepper, sliced
  - 1 green bell pepper, sliced
  - 1 red onion, sliced
  - 1 tablespoon olive oil
  - Salt and pepper to taste

- **For garnish:**
  - Fresh cilantro
  - Lime wedges

Instructions:

1. Marinate the chicken:
   - In a bowl, mix the olive oil, cumin, chili powder, paprika, garlic powder, salt, pepper, and lime juice.
   - Add the chicken strips to the marinade and let them sit for at least 15-20 minutes to absorb the flavors.

2. Grill the chicken:

- Heat a grill or grill pan over medium-high heat.
- Grill the chicken strips for 5-7 minutes per side until fully cooked and slightly charred. Remove from the grill and set aside.

3. Cook the vegetables:
   - In a large skillet, heat 1 tablespoon of olive oil over medium heat.
   - Add the sliced bell peppers and onions to the skillet, season with salt and pepper, and cook for 8-10 minutes, stirring occasionally, until the vegetables are soft and slightly caramelized.

4. Combine and serve:
   - Add the grilled chicken back to the skillet with the vegetables and toss to combine.
   - Serve the fajita mixture hot, garnished with fresh cilantro and lime wedges.

Nutritional Info (Per Serving):
Calories: 350 kcal per serving
Fats: 14 g (3 g saturated)
Carbohydrates: 20 g (5 g fiber, 4 g sugar)
Protein: 35 g

Key Nutrients: Protein, vitamin C, fiber, and potassium

Tips: Serve with warm gluten-free tortillas or cauliflower rice for a lighter option. Add guacamole or sour cream for extra richness.

10. Japanese Grilled Mackerel with Rice and Vegetables

This dish is rich in iodine and omega-3 fatty acids from the mackerel, which support heart and thyroid health. The fresh vegetables provide a wealth of vitamins and minerals, while the rice offers a gluten-free carbohydrate option for sustained energy.

Prep Time: 15 minutes
Cooking Time: 20 minutes
Servings: 2

Ingredients:
- 2 fillets of mackerel (about 200g each)
- 1 tbsp olive oil
- 2 tbsp soy-free tamari sauce
- 1 tbsp mirin (sweet rice wine)
- 1 tbsp rice vinegar
- 1 clove garlic, minced
- 1 tsp fresh ginger, grated
- 1 cup rice
- 1 cup water
- 1 small cucumber, sliced
- 1 small carrot, sliced
- 1 small tomato
- 1 tbsp pickled vegetables (optional)
- 1 tbsp seaweed, thinly sliced for garnish
- Salt and pepper to taste

Instructions:

1. Marinate the Mackerel: In a small bowl, mix tamari sauce, mirin, rice vinegar, garlic, ginger, and olive oil. Place the mackerel fillets in a shallow dish and pour the marinade over them. Let it marinate for at least 20 minutes.

2. Cook the Rice: Rinse the rice under cold water until the water runs clear. Place it in a pot with 1 cup of water and bring to a boil. Reduce the heat, cover, and let it simmer for about 15-20 minutes or until the rice is cooked. Let it sit covered for an additional 10 minutes to steam.

3. Grill the Mackerel: Preheat a grill or stovetop grill pan over medium-high heat. Remove the mackerel fillets from the marinade and grill for 4-5 minutes on each side, or until the fish is cooked through and slightly charred.

4. Prepare the Vegetables: Arrange the cucumber slices, carrot slices, and tomato on a plate. You can also add pickled vegetables for extra flavor if desired.

5. Assemble the Dish: Serve the grilled mackerel alongside the steamed rice and vegetables. Garnish with sliced seaweed and a drizzle of the leftover marinade.

Nutritional Info (Per Serving):
Calories: 540 kcal per serving
Fats: 22 g (6 g saturated)
Carbohydrates: 50 g (4 g fiber, 6 g sugar)
Protein: 34 g

Key Nutrients: Iodine, omega-3s, vitamin A, and selenium

Tips: Use fresh mackerel for the best flavor, and garnish with sesame seeds for added texture. Add pickled ginger as a side for a traditional touch.

11. Savory Shrimp Soup

This soup is rich in protein from shrimp, which is low in calories and high in iodine. The inclusion of tomatoes provides antioxidants like vitamin C, while the potatoes offer complex carbohydrates and potassium, supporting energy levels and heart health.

Prep Time: 15 minutes
Cooking Time: 30 minutes
Servings: 4

Ingredients:
- 1 lb (450g) shrimp, peeled and deveined
- 2 medium potatoes, diced
- 1 small onion, diced
- 2 cloves garlic, minced
- 1 celery stalk, chopped
- 1 can (14 oz) diced tomatoes
- 4 cups vegetable or seafood broth
- 1/2 tsp paprika
- 1/2 tsp cumin
- 1/4 tsp cayenne pepper (optional)
- Salt and pepper to taste
- 2 tbsp olive oil
- Fresh parsley, chopped for garnish
- 1 bay leaf
- 1/2 lemon for squeezing

Instructions:
1. Sauté the Vegetables: In a large pot, heat the olive oil over medium heat. Add the onion, garlic, and celery. Sauté for 4-5 minutes until the vegetables are soft and fragrant.
2. Add Potatoes and Seasonings: Add the diced potatoes, paprika, cumin, cayenne (if using), and bay leaf. Stir to combine and cook for 2 minutes.
3. Add Broth and Tomatoes: Pour in the vegetable or seafood broth and diced tomatoes. Bring to a boil, then reduce the heat and simmer for 15-20 minutes, or until the potatoes are tender.
4. Cook the Shrimp: Add the shrimp to the pot and cook for 4-5 minutes, or until they turn pink and opaque.
5. Season and Serve: Remove the bay leaf, season with salt and pepper to taste, and squeeze lemon juice over the soup. Garnish with fresh parsley and serve hot.

Nutritional Info (Per Serving):

Calories: 300 kcal per serving

Fats: 10 g (2 g saturated)

Carbohydrates: 35 g (5 g fiber, 5 g sugar)

Protein: 25 g

Key Nutrients: Iodine, selenium, potassium, and vitamin C

Tips: Add a dash of chili flakes for some heat or serve with a squeeze of lime for added brightness.

12. Chicken and Vegetable Stir-Fry

This stir-fry provides a balance of lean protein from the chicken and fiber-rich vegetables, which are packed with vitamins and minerals like vitamin C and potassium. Tamari or coconut aminos offer a thyroid-friendly alternative to soy sauce.

Prep Time: 15 minutes
Cooking Time: 10 minutes
Servings: 4

Ingredients:

- 2 chicken breasts, diced
- 1 zucchini, chopped
- 1 red bell pepper, chopped
- 1 green bell pepper, chopped
- 1 tablespoon olive oil
- 2 garlic cloves, minced
- 2 tablespoons tamari or coconut aminos (soy-free alternative)
- 1 tablespoon rice vinegar
- 1 teaspoon sesame seeds (optional)
- 1/2 teaspoon chili flakes (optional, for heat)
- Salt and pepper to taste
- Cooked jasmine rice (for serving)

Instructions:

1. Prepare the Chicken:
   - Heat olive oil in a large skillet or wok over medium-high heat. Add diced chicken and cook for 5-7 minutes, until the chicken is browned and cooked through. Remove from the skillet and set aside.

2. Stir-Fry the Vegetables:
   - In the same skillet, add garlic and stir-fry for about 30 seconds until fragrant. Add the zucchini, red bell pepper, and green bell pepper. Stir-fry for about 5 minutes until the vegetables are slightly softened but still have a bit of crunch.

3. Combine and Season:
   - Return the chicken to the skillet with the vegetables. Add tamari (or coconut aminos), rice vinegar, and chili flakes (if using). Stir everything together and cook for another 2-3 minutes to combine the flavors.

4. Serve:
   - Serve the stir-fry over jasmine rice and garnish with sesame seeds for extra flavor and crunch.

Nutritional Info (Per Serving):
Calories: 350 kcal per serving
Fats: 10 g (2 g saturated)
Carbohydrates: 30 g (4 g fiber, 5 g sugar)
Protein: 35 g

Key Nutrients: Protein, vitamin C, potassium, and fiber

Tips: Add crushed cashews for extra crunch and flavor. Use tamari or coconut aminos to keep the dish gluten-free.

13. Creamy Mushroom Risotto

Mushrooms are packed with antioxidants and B vitamins, that support energy metabolism and immune function. Arborio rice provides a source of slow-digesting carbohydrates, making this dish both satisfying and nourishing.

Prep Time: 10 minutes
Cooking Time: 30 minutes
Servings: 4

Ingredients:
- 1 cup Arborio rice
- 1 tablespoon olive oil
- 1 small onion, finely chopped
- 2 garlic cloves, minced
- 1 cup mushrooms, sliced (use cremini, button, or shiitake)
- 4 cups low-sodium vegetable broth (or chicken broth)
- 1/2 cup dry white wine
- 1/2 cup Parmesan cheese, grated
- 2 tablespoons unsalted butter
- Fresh parsley, chopped (for garnish)
- Salt and pepper to taste

Instructions:

1. Sauté the Mushrooms:
   Heat olive oil in a large skillet over medium heat. Add the chopped onions and sauté for 3-4 minutes until softened. Add garlic and cook for another minute. Add the mushrooms and cook until they release their moisture and become golden brown, about 5 minutes. Remove from the pan and set aside.

2. Cook the Risotto:
   In the same pan, add the Arborio rice and cook for 1-2 minutes, stirring constantly, until the rice is lightly toasted. Pour in the white wine and let it simmer, stirring, until the wine is mostly absorbed by the rice.

3. Add Broth Gradually:
   Start adding the warm broth one ladle at a time, stirring frequently. Allow the rice to absorb most of the broth before adding more. Continue this process for about 18-20 minutes until the rice is tender and creamy but still slightly al dente.

4. Finish the Dish:
   Stir in the sautéed mushrooms, butter, and grated Parmesan cheese. Mix well until the risotto becomes creamy and well combined. Season with salt and pepper to taste.

5. Serve:
   Garnish with freshly chopped parsley and a sprinkle of Parmesan. Serve warm.

Nutritional Info (Per Serving):
Calories: 410 kcal per serving
Fats: 14 g (6 g saturated)
Carbohydrates: 55 g (4 g fiber, 5 g sugar)
Protein: 12 g

Key Nutrients: Selenium, B vitamins, magnesium, and fiber

Tips: Use a mix of mushrooms like shiitake, cremini, and portobello for depth of flavor. Stir continuously to achieve the perfect creamy texture.

14. Shredded Beef Tacos

This dish is packed with high-quality protein from the beef, the tomatoes and avocado provide a healthy dose of vitamins, antioxidants, and healthy fats to support overall well-being.

Prep Time: 20 minutes
Cooking Time: 2-3 hours
Servings: 8 tacos

Ingredients:
- 1 lb beef chuck roast
- 1 tablespoon olive oil
- 1 onion, diced
- 2 garlic cloves, minced
- 1 teaspoon ground cumin
- 1 teaspoon chili powder
- 1 teaspoon paprika
- 1/2 teaspoon oregano
- Salt and pepper to taste
- 1 cup beef broth
- 8 small corn tortillas
- Diced tomatoes, onions, cilantro, and avocado (for toppings)
- Lime wedges (for serving)

Instructions:

1. Prepare the Beef:
   Heat olive oil in a large pot or Dutch oven over medium heat. Season the beef chuck roast with salt, pepper, cumin, chili powder, paprika, and oregano. Sear the beef on all sides until browned, about 4-5 minutes per side. Remove the beef and set aside.

2. Cook the Beef:
   In the same pot, add the diced onion and garlic. Sauté until soft and fragrant, about 3-4 minutes. Add the beef back to the pot and pour in the beef broth. Bring to a simmer, then cover and cook on low heat for 2-3 hours, until the beef is tender and easily shredded with a fork.

3. Shred the Beef:
   Remove the beef from the pot and shred it using two forks. If needed, add a little bit of the cooking liquid to keep the meat moist.

4. Assemble the Tacos:

Warm the corn tortillas in a dry skillet or over an open flame until they are slightly charred. Fill each tortilla with a generous portion of shredded beef and top with diced tomatoes, onions, cilantro, and avocado. Serve with lime wedges on the side for extra flavor.

Nutritional Info (Per Serving):
Calories: 370 kcal per taco
Fats: 15 g (4 g saturated)
Carbohydrates: 26 g (4 g fiber, 2 g sugar)
Protein: 30 g

Key Nutrients: Iron, zinc, protein, and vitamin C

Tips: Use a slow cooker for convenience and enhanced flavor. Pair with a side of guacamole or salsa for a complete meal.

15. Lamb Kebab and Vegetable Skewers

Lamb provides high-quality protein and essential nutrients like zinc and iron, the colorful vegetables offer a variety of vitamins, minerals, and antioxidants.

Prep Time: 30 minutes
Cooking Time: 10 minutes
Servings: 4

Ingredients:
- 500g lamb chunks (cut into 1-inch cubes)
- 1 red bell pepper, cut into squares
- 1 yellow bell pepper, cut into squares
- 1 green bell pepper, cut into squares
- 1 zucchini, sliced
- 1 red onion, cut into chunks
- 2 tbsp olive oil
- 2 tbsp lemon juice
- 2 garlic cloves, minced
- 1 tsp cumin powder
- 1 tsp smoked paprika
- Fresh parsley for garnish
- Salt and pepper to taste

Instructions:
1. Prepare the Marinade: In a bowl, mix olive oil, lemon juice, garlic, cumin, paprika, salt, and pepper. Add the lamb chunks and let marinate for at least 30 minutes (or overnight for more flavor).
2. Assemble the Skewers: Thread the marinated lamb, bell peppers, zucchini, and onion onto skewers, alternating the pieces.
3. Grill: Heat the grill to medium-high. Place the skewers on the grill and cook for about 8-10 minutes, turning occasionally, until the lamb is browned and vegetables are charred.
4. Serve: Garnish with fresh parsley and serve warm with your choice of side, such as rice or salad.

Nutritional Info (Per Serving):
Calories: 450 kcal per skewer
Fats: 30 g (8 g saturated)
Carbohydrates: 15 g (4 g fiber, 6 g sugar)
Protein: 30 g

Key Nutrients: Iron, zinc, vitamin C, and fiber

Tips: Marinate the lamb overnight for enhanced flavor. Serve with a side of hummus or a fresh salad.

16. Lemon Garlic Baked Cod

Cod is a lean source of protein rich in iodine. The inclusion of olive oil and garlic provides healthy fats and antioxidants to support overall well-being.

Prep Time: 10 minutes
Cooking Time: 15 minutes
Servings: 2

Ingredients:
- 2 large cod fillets
- 2 tbsp olive oil
- 2 garlic cloves, minced
- 1 lemon, sliced
- 1 tsp lemon zest
- 1 tsp paprika
- Fresh thyme leaves
- Salt and pepper to taste

Instructions:
1. Preheat the Oven: Set the oven to 200°C (400°F).
2. Prepare the Cod: Place the cod fillets in a baking dish. Drizzle with olive oil and season with salt, pepper, paprika, and lemon zest. Spread minced garlic on top.
3. Add Lemon and Herbs: Lay lemon slices over the cod fillets and sprinkle fresh thyme leaves on top.
4. Bake: Bake the cod in the oven for 12-15 minutes, or until it flakes easily with a fork.
5. Serve: Garnish with extra thyme and a squeeze of lemon juice. Serve with roasted vegetables or a fresh green salad.

Nutritional Info (Per Serving):
Calories: 250 kcal per serving
Fats: 13 g (3 g saturated)
Carbohydrates: 2 g (0 g fiber, 0 g sugar)
Protein: 30 g

Key Nutrients: Iodine, selenium, omega-3s, and vitamin C

Tips: Serve with a side of steamed green beans or roasted sweet potatoes for a balanced meal.

17. Gourmet Steak Dinner with Mashed Sweet Potatoes and Sautéed Kale

This dish is packed with high-quality protein from the steak, providing essential amino acids. The sweet potatoes are rich in fiber and beta-carotene, which support thyroid health and immune function. The kale offers a hefty dose of vitamins A, C, and K, boosting antioxidant levels.

Prep Time: 15 minutes
Cooking Time: 25 minutes
Servings: 2

Ingredients:
- 2 beef filet mignon steaks (6 oz each)
- 2 cups sweet potatoes, peeled and cubed
- 1 bunch kale, stems removed, chopped
- 2 tbsp olive oil, divided
- 2 tbsp unsalted butter
- 2 garlic cloves, minced
- 1/2 cup beef broth
- Salt and pepper to taste
- Fresh thyme or microgreens for garnish (optional)
- 1 tbsp sesame seeds (optional)

Instructions:

1. Prepare the Mashed Sweet Potatoes:
   - Bring a pot of water to boil. Add cubed sweet potatoes and cook for about 10-12 minutes until tender. Drain and mash with butter, salt, and pepper to taste. Set aside.

2. Cook the Kale:
   - In a large pan, heat 1 tbsp of olive oil over medium heat. Add the minced garlic and sauté for 1 minute. Add the kale and cook for 5-7 minutes, stirring occasionally until wilted. Season with salt and pepper, then set aside.

3. Sear the Steaks:
   - Season the steaks generously with salt and pepper. Heat the remaining olive oil in a cast-iron skillet over medium-high heat. Sear the steaks for 3-4 minutes on each side for medium-rare, or cook longer depending on your preference. Remove the steaks from the skillet and let them rest.

4. Make the Sauce:
   - In the same skillet, add beef broth and bring to a simmer, scraping up the browned bits. Let the sauce reduce by half, about 5 minutes.

5. Assemble the Dish:
   - On a plate, spread the mashed sweet potatoes as a base. Top with the sautéed kale, then place the filet mignon on top. Drizzle the reduced sauce over the steak and garnish with sesame seeds and fresh thyme or microgreens.

Nutritional Info (Per Serving):
Calories: 550 kcal per serving
Fats: 28 g (10 g saturated)
Carbohydrates: 35 g (7 g fiber, 8 g sugar)
Protein: 40 g

Key Nutrients: Protein, vitamin A, vitamin K, and beta-carotene

Tips: Let the steak rest for a few minutes after cooking to retain its juices. Garnish with sesame seeds for added texture.

18. Braised Chicken with Pearl Onions and Mushrooms

This dish provides lean protein from the chicken, which supports muscle growth and repair. The pearl onions are rich in vitamin C and fiber, while mushrooms provide B vitamins and selenium, promoting thyroid health and boosting the immune system.

Prep Time: 15 minutes
Cooking Time: 40 minutes
Servings: 4

Ingredients:
  - 4 bone-in chicken thighs, skin on
  - 1 tablespoon olive oil
  - 1 tablespoon butter
  - 1 cup pearl onions, peeled
  - 2 cups mushrooms, sliced (baby bella or cremini work well)
  - 2 cloves garlic, minced
  - 1/2 cup red wine (optional)
  - 1 cup chicken broth
  - 2 sprigs fresh thyme
  - 1 bay leaf
  - Salt and pepper to taste

Instructions:

1. Sear the chicken:
   - Season the chicken thighs with salt and pepper.
   - Heat olive oil and butter in a large skillet or Dutch oven over medium-high heat.
   - Sear the chicken thighs skin-side down until golden brown, about 4-5 minutes. Flip and sear the other side for 2-3 minutes. Remove from the skillet and set aside.

2. Cook the vegetables:
   - In the same skillet, add the pearl onions and mushrooms. Cook for 3-4 minutes until they begin to soften.
   - Add the minced garlic and cook for another minute, being careful not to burn it.

3. Deglaze and braise:
   - Pour in the red wine (if using) and let it reduce by half.
   - Add the chicken broth, thyme, and bay leaf to the skillet. Stir to combine.
   - Return the chicken thighs to the skillet, skin-side up, and bring the liquid to a simmer.

- Reduce the heat to low, cover, and let the chicken braise for 30-40 minutes, or until the chicken is cooked through and tender.

4. Serve:
   - Remove the thyme sprigs and bay leaf before serving.
   - Plate the chicken with the pearl onions, mushrooms, and sauce. Garnish with fresh thyme for extra flavor.

Nutritional Info (Per Serving):
Calories: 450 kcal per serving
Fats: 30 g (8 g saturated)
Carbohydrates: 15 g (3 g fiber, 4 g sugar)
Protein: 35 g

Key Nutrients: Selenium, B vitamins, protein, and antioxidants

Tips: Serve with a side of crusty gluten-free bread or over mashed potatoes for a hearty meal.

19. Crispy Crusted Fish

This dish is rich in omega-3 fatty acids from the fish, the almond flour adds a boost of healthy fats.

Prep Time: 15 minutes
Cooking Time: 10-15 minutes
Servings: 2

Ingredients:
- 2 white fish fillets (such as cod or haddock)
- 1/2 cup almond flour
- 1 egg, beaten
- 1 tsp garlic powder
- 1 tsp smoked paprika
- 1/2 tsp black pepper
- 1/2 tsp salt
- Lemon wedges, for serving
- Fresh parsley, chopped (optional, for garnish)

Instructions:

1. Prepare the Fish: Preheat your air fryer to 375°F (190°C) or oven to 400°F (200°C). Pat the fish fillets dry with paper towels.

2. Make the Coating: In a shallow dish, combine the almond flour, garlic powder, smoked paprika, salt, and black pepper. Stir well.

3. Coat the Fish: Dip each fish fillet into the beaten egg. Press each fillet into the mixture, coating both sides evenly.

4. Cook the Fish:
   - For Air Fryer: Place the fish fillets in the air fryer basket, making sure they don't overlap. Air fry for 8-10 minutes, flipping halfway through, until golden brown and crispy.
   - For Oven: Place the fish on a parchment-lined baking sheet and bake for 12-15 minutes, or until the crust is golden and the fish flakes easily with a fork.

5. Serve: Garnish with fresh parsley and serve with lemon wedges on the side for a burst of freshness.

Nutritional Info (Per Serving):
Calories: 320 kcal per serving
Fats: 18 g (3 g saturated)
Carbohydrates: 6 g (2 g fiber, 1 g sugar)
Protein: 35 g

Key Nutrients: Omega-3s, healthy fats, selenium, and vitamin E

Tips: Serve with a side of coleslaw or a light green salad. For a spicier kick, add chili powder to the coating mixture.

20. Herb-Roasted Whole Chicken with Crispy Potatoes

This dish is rich in protein from the chicken, to support muscle repair and immune function. The addition of fresh herbs offers antioxidants and anti-inflammatory properties, while the potatoes provide essential fiber and vitamins.

Prep Time: 20 minutes
Cooking Time: 1 hour 20 minutes
Servings: 6

Ingredients:
- 1 whole chicken (about 4-5 lbs)
- 2 tbsp olive oil
- 2 tbsp fresh rosemary, chopped
- 2 tbsp fresh thyme, chopped
- 4 garlic cloves, minced
- 1 lemon, halved
- Salt and pepper to taste
- 1.5 lbs baby potatoes, halved
- 2 tbsp butter, melted
- Fresh parsley, chopped (for garnish)

Instructions:

1. Prepare the Chicken: Preheat the oven to 425°F (220°C). Pat the chicken dry with paper towels. Rub the chicken all over with olive oil, then season generously with salt, pepper, rosemary, thyme, and minced garlic. Place the lemon halves inside the cavity of the chicken.

2. Roast the Chicken: Place the chicken breast-side up on a roasting pan or baking dish. Roast for about 1 hour and 20 minutes, or until the internal temperature reaches 165°F (74°C) in the thickest part of the thigh. Baste the chicken with its juices halfway through cooking.

3. Prepare the Potatoes: In a bowl, toss the halved baby potatoes with melted butter, salt, and pepper. After the chicken has been roasting for 40 minutes, add the potatoes around the chicken in the same pan.

4. Finish and Serve: Once the chicken is done, remove it from the oven and let it rest for 10 minutes before carving. Garnish with fresh parsley and serve alongside the crispy roasted potatoes.

Nutritional Info (Per Serving):

Calories: 530 kcal per serving

Fats: 28g (9g saturated)

Carbohydrates: 25g (4g fiber, 3g sugar)

Protein: 45g

Key Nutrients: Protein, vitamin C, fiber, potassium, antioxidants

Tips: Use a meat thermometer to ensure the chicken is fully cooked without overbaking. Serve with a side of steamed green beans or roasted carrots for a complete meal.

21. Herb-Crusted Rack of Lamb with Mashed Potatoes

Lamb provides essential minerals like zinc and iron, while fresh herbs and creamy mashed potatoes offer antioxidants and energy-sustaining carbohydrates.

Prep Time: 20 minutes
Cooking Time: 35 minutes
Servings: 4

Ingredients:
- **For the lamb:**
  - 1 rack of lamb (about 8 ribs)
  - 2 tablespoons olive oil
  - 2 tablespoons Dijon mustard
  - 2 cloves garlic, minced
  - 2 tablespoons fresh rosemary, chopped
  - 1 tablespoon fresh thyme, chopped
  - Salt and pepper to taste

- **For the mashed potatoes:**
  - 4 large potatoes, peeled and cubed
  - 4 tablespoons butter
  - 1/2 cup milk (or more, to desired creaminess)
  - Salt and pepper to taste

Instructions:

1. Prepare the lamb:
   - Preheat your oven to 400°F (200°C).
   - Season the rack of lamb with salt and pepper.
   - Heat the olive oil in a skillet over medium-high heat and sear the lamb for 2-3 minutes on each side until browned. Remove from heat and let cool slightly.

2. Make the herb crust:
   - In a small bowl, mix the minced garlic, rosemary, thyme, and Dijon mustard.
   - Rub the herb mixture all over the lamb, coating it evenly.

3. Roast the lamb:
   - Place the lamb in a roasting pan and roast in the preheated oven for 15-20 minutes for medium-rare, or until the internal temperature reaches 135°F (57°C).
   - Let the lamb rest for 5-10 minutes before carving.

4. Prepare the mashed potatoes:
   - While the lamb is roasting, boil the potatoes in salted water until tender, about 15 minutes.
   - Drain the potatoes, add the butter and milk, and mash until smooth.
   - Season with salt and pepper to taste.

5. Serve:
   - Slice the rack of lamb into individual chops.
   - Serve the herb-crusted lamb with creamy mashed potatoes, and garnish with extra rosemary if desired.

Nutritional Info (Per Serving):
Calories: 600 kcal per serving
Fats: 35g (12g saturated)
Carbohydrates: 45g (6g fiber, 3g sugar)
Protein: 40g

Key Nutrients: Iron, zinc, protein, vitamin B12

Tips: Let the lamb rest for 10 minutes after roasting to ensure juicy and tender meat. Pair with roasted asparagus or a fresh green salad for added nutrients.

22. Beef Fajitas with Guacamole

This dish is rich in protein and healthy fats from the beef and avocado, while the bell peppers provide a good source of vitamin C, all beneficial for maintaining healthy skin and immune function.

Prep Time: 20 minutes
Cooking Time: 20 minutes
Servings: 4

Ingredients:
- 500g (1 lb) beef strips (flank or skirt steak)
- 2 bell peppers (red and yellow), sliced
- 1 onion, sliced
- 2 tbsp olive oil
- 1 tsp ground cumin
- 1 tsp smoked paprika
- 1 tsp garlic powder
- Salt and pepper to taste
- 4 small corn tortillas
- Fresh lime wedges for garnish

Guacamole:
- 2 ripe avocados
- 1 small tomato, diced
- 1 small onion, finely chopped
- Juice of 1 lime
- Salt to taste

Instructions:

1. Marinate the Beef: In a bowl, combine the beef strips with olive oil, cumin, paprika, garlic powder, salt, and pepper. Let it marinate for 15-20 minutes.
2. Cook the Vegetables: Heat a large skillet over medium-high heat. Add a little olive oil and sauté the bell peppers and onions until softened, about 5-6 minutes. Remove from the pan and set aside.
3. Cook the Beef: In the same skillet, cook the beef strips for about 3-4 minutes on each side until they're nicely browned.
4. Make the Guacamole: Mash the avocados in a bowl, then mix in the diced tomato, onion, lime juice, and salt.
5. Assemble the Fajitas: Warm the tortillas in a dry skillet. Layer the cooked beef, sautéed vegetables, and a generous dollop of guacamole on each tortilla.

6. Serve: Garnish with fresh lime wedges and enjoy!

Nutritional Info (Per Serving):
Calories: 350 kcal per tortilla
Fats: 18g (6g saturated)
Carbohydrates: 28g (5g fiber, 4g sugar)
Protein: 25g

Key Nutrients: Iron, vitamin C, healthy fats, protein

Tips: Use gluten-free tortillas, serve with a side of salsa or black beans for a more filling meal.

23. Grilled Steak with Roasted Sweet Potatoes and Fresh Arugula Salad

This meal is rich in high-quality protein from the steak. Sweet potatoes provide essential vitamins like vitamin A and fiber, which are great for digestion, while arugula is packed with antioxidants and vitamins, supporting overall health.

Prep Time: 20 minutes
Cooking Time: 30 minutes
Servings: 4

Ingredients:
- 1 lb ribeye or sirloin steak
- 2 medium sweet potatoes, peeled and cut into cubes
- 2 cups fresh arugula
- 1 tbsp olive oil
- 1 tsp paprika
- 1 tsp garlic powder
- Salt and pepper to taste

Instructions:

1. Roast the Sweet Potatoes: Preheat your oven to 400°F (200°C). Toss the sweet potato cubes with olive oil, paprika, garlic powder, salt, and pepper. Spread them evenly on a baking sheet and roast for 25-30 minutes, or until golden and tender, turning halfway through.

2. Grill the Steak: While the sweet potatoes are roasting, heat your grill or grill pan to high. Season the steak generously with salt and pepper. Grill for 4-5 minutes per side for medium-rare, or to your desired doneness. Remove from the grill and let it rest for 5 minutes before slicing.

3. Prepare the Salad: Toss the fresh arugula with a squeeze of lemon juice and a drizzle of olive oil. Add a pinch of salt for taste.

4. Serve: Plate the sliced steak with roasted sweet potatoes and arugula salad on the side.

Nutritional Info (Per Serving):
Calories: 640 kcal per serving
Fats: 33g (12g saturated)
Carbohydrates: 42g (7g fiber, 10g sugar)
Protein: 43g

Key Nutrients: Protein, vitamin A, fiber, antioxidants

Tips: Allow the steak to rest for 5 minutes after grilling to retain its juices.

24. Roasted Duck with Rosemary, Potatoes, and Carrots

Duck provides high-quality protein and essential fatty acids, while rosemary and nutrient-rich vegetables offer antioxidants and fiber for optimal health.

Prep Time: 30 minutes
Cooking Time: 2 hours
Servings: 6

Ingredients:
- **For the duck:**
  - 1 whole duck (about 4-5 pounds)
  - 2 tablespoons olive oil
  - 2 sprigs fresh rosemary
  - 4 cloves garlic, minced
  - Salt and pepper to taste
  - 1 tablespoon honey (optional, for glazing)

- **For the vegetables:**
  - 1 pound baby potatoes, halved
  - 4 large carrots, peeled and cut into large chunks
  - 1 tablespoon olive oil
  - 2 sprigs fresh rosemary
  - Salt and pepper to taste

Instructions:

1. Prepare the duck:
   - Preheat the oven to 375°F (190°C).
   - Pat the duck dry with paper towels and season the cavity generously with salt, pepper, and minced garlic. Stuff the cavity with rosemary sprigs.
   - Rub the outside of the duck with olive oil and season with salt and pepper. Optionally, brush the duck with honey for added sweetness and a crisp glaze.

2. Roast the duck:
   - Place the duck breast-side up in a roasting pan. Roast for 1.5 to 2 hours, or until the internal temperature reaches 165°F (74°C) and the skin is golden brown and crispy.
   - During the last 30 minutes of roasting, baste the duck with its own juices to keep it moist.

3. Prepare the vegetables:

- While the duck is roasting, toss the potatoes and carrots with olive oil, rosemary, salt, and pepper.
   - Spread the vegetables on a baking sheet in a single layer.

4. Roast the vegetables:
   - About 45 minutes before the duck is done, place the prepared vegetables in the oven. Roast for 35-40 minutes, or until golden and tender, stirring halfway through.

5. Serve:
   - Remove the duck from the oven and let it rest for 10 minutes before carving.
   - Serve the roasted duck alongside the potatoes and carrots, garnished with fresh rosemary for a beautiful presentation.

Nutritional Info (Per Serving):
Calories: 650 kcal per serving
Fats: 40g (12g saturated)
Carbohydrates: 35g (6g fiber, 8g sugar)
Protein: 40g

Key Nutrients: Protein, vitamin A, antioxidants, omega-3s

Tips: For extra crispy skin, pat the duck dry thoroughly before roasting. Pair with a side of cranberry sauce for a festive touch.

25. Shrimp Paella

This Shrimp Paella is rich in iodine, the addition of bell peppers, rich in vitamin C, supports the absorption of other nutrients that contribute to overall thyroid well-being.. The saffron and garlic add antioxidants, making it a nutritious and flavorful meal.

Prep Time: 15 minutes
Cooking Time: 30 minutes
Servings: 6

Ingredients:
- 1 lb large shrimp, peeled and deveined
- 1 1/2 cups Arborio rice or paella rice
- 1 red bell pepper, diced
- 1 yellow bell pepper, diced
- 1 green bell pepper, diced
- 1 medium onion, chopped
- 2 garlic cloves, minced
- 1 tsp smoked paprika
- 1/2 tsp saffron threads
- 4 cups vegetable or seafood broth
- 1 can (14 oz) diced tomatoes, drained
- 1/2 cup frozen peas
- 2 tbsp olive oil
- Salt and pepper to taste
- Fresh parsley for garnish

Instructions:

1. Prepare the Base:
   Heat the olive oil in a large paella pan or wide skillet over medium heat. Add the onion and garlic, and sauté for 3-4 minutes until softened. Stir in the red, yellow, and green bell peppers, and continue cooking for another 5 minutes until the vegetables are tender.

2. Add the Rice:
   Stir in the Arborio rice, ensuring it's coated with the oil and mixed with the vegetables. Toast the rice for 2 minutes, then add the smoked paprika and saffron. Pour in the broth, and bring the mixture to a simmer. Cover the pan and reduce heat to low. Let it cook for 15 minutes, stirring occasionally.

3. Add the Shrimp and Peas:

After the rice has cooked, stir in the drained tomatoes and frozen peas. Place the shrimp on top of the rice, cover again, and cook for another 5-7 minutes, until the shrimp are pink and cooked through.

4. Finish and Serve:

Remove the pan from heat and let it sit, covered, for 5 minutes. Garnish with fresh parsley before serving.

Nutritional Info (Per Serving):

Calories: 420 kcal per serving
Fats: 12g (3g saturated)
Carbohydrates: 50g (5g fiber, 6g sugar)
Protein: 28g

Key Nutrients: Iodine, selenium, vitamin C, protein

Tips: Use saffron sparingly for its distinct flavor and vibrant color. Serve with a lemon wedge for added brightness.

Chapter 8: Snacks and Appetizers

On those busy days when you crave something quick, nutritious, and kind to your thyroid, snacks and appetizers can be your delightful mini-meals! These recipes are all about quick and easy preparation, ensuring you get plenty of nutrients and delicious flavors, all while being kind to your thyroid health!

1. Almond Butter and Apple Slices

Apples provide fiber to support digestion, while almond butter is rich in magnesium, which aids in thyroid hormone production.

Prep time: 5 minutes
Serving: 1

Ingredients:
- 1 medium apple, sliced
- 2 tbsp almond butter (unsweetened)

Instructions:
1. Slice the apple into wedges.
2. Serve with a generous dollop of almond butter for dipping.

Nutritional Info (Per Serving):
Calories: 190 kcal
Fats: 9 g (1 g saturated)
Carbohydrates: 25 g (4 g fiber, 19 g sugar)
Protein: 4 g

Key nutrients: Vitamin C, Potassium, Magnesium

2. Sliced Avocado with Lemon and Sea Salt

Avocados provide healthy monounsaturated fats and antioxidants that reduce inflammation and support thyroid function.

Prep time: 5 minutes
Serving: 1

Ingredients:
- 1 ripe avocado
- 1/2 lemon, juiced
- Sea salt to taste
- Black pepper

Instructions:
1. Slice the avocado and drizzle with lemon juice.
2. Sprinkle with sea salt and black pepper and enjoy immediately.

Nutritional Info (Per Serving):
Calories: 160 kcal
Fats: 15 g (2 g saturated)
Carbohydrates: 8 g (6 g fiber, 1 g sugar)
Protein: 2 g

Key nutrients: Vitamin E, Potassium, Magnesium

3. Boiled Eggs with Olive Oil Drizzle

This high-protein, thyroid-friendly snack is packed with iodine and selenium.

Prep time: 10 minutes
Serving: 1

Ingredients:
- 2 boiled eggs
- 1 tsp olive oil
- A pinch of salt and pepper

Instructions:
1. Boil the eggs to your preferred consistency.
2. Once peeled, drizzle with olive oil and sprinkle with salt and pepper.

Nutritional Info (Per Serving):

Calories: 180 kcal
Fats: 14 g (3.5 g saturated)
Carbohydrates: 1 g (0 g fiber, 0 g sugar)
Protein: 12 g

Key nutrients: Selenium, Choline, Vitamin B12

4. Brazil Nuts and Blueberries

This simple mix offers a balance of antioxidants and selenium (Brazil nuts are the richest natural source of selenium).

Prep time: 2 minutes
Serving: 1

Ingredients:
- 5 Brazil nuts
- 1/4 cup fresh blueberries

Instructions:
1. Combine Brazil nuts with blueberries in a small bowl and enjoy.

Nutritional Info (Per Serving):
Calories: 120 kcal
Fats: 9 g (1 g saturated)
Carbohydrates: 8 g (2 g fiber, 6 g sugar)
Protein: 2 g

Key nutrients: Selenium, Antioxidants, Vitamin C

5. Avocado and Cherry Tomato Cup

Avocados provide healthy fats, particularly monounsaturated fats, while cherry tomatoes are rich in vitamin C and antioxidants to boost your immune system.

Prep time: 5 minutes
Serving: 1

Ingredients:
- 1 ripe avocado, sliced
- A handful of cherry tomatoes, halved
- A drizzle of extra virgin olive oil
- A pinch of sea salt
- Freshly ground black pepper

Instructions:
1. In a small cup or bowl, arrange the avocado slices neatly.
2. Top with halved cherry tomatoes.
3. Drizzle with olive oil and sprinkle a pinch of sea salt and freshly ground black pepper on top.
4. Serve immediately for a refreshing, nutrient-packed snack.

Nutritional Info (Per Serving):
Calories: 220 kcal
Fats: 18 g (2.5 g saturated)
Carbohydrates: 14 g (7 g fiber, 4 g sugar)
Protein: 3 g

Key nutrients: Vitamin C, Vitamin E, Potassium

6. Thyroid-Boosting Smoothie

This smoothie is full of thyroid-supporting ingredients, coconut oil contains medium-chain fatty acids, which support thyroid function, while spinach and berries provide vitamins and antioxidants.

Prep time: 5 minutes
Serving: 1

Ingredients:
- 1 cup spinach
- 1/2 cup mixed berries (blueberries, strawberries)
- 1 tbsp coconut oil
- 1/2 cup unsweetened almond milk
- 1 tsp chia seeds

Instructions:
1. Blend all the ingredients until smooth.
2. Serve immediately for a nutrient-packed snack.

Nutritional Info (Per Serving):
Calories: 220 kcal
Fats: 16 g (6 g saturated)
Carbohydrates: 16 g (4 g fiber, 8 g sugar)
Protein: 4 g

Key nutrients: Omega-3 Fatty Acids, Antioxidants, Vitamin C

7. Coconut Yogurt with Walnuts and Honey

Coconut yogurt provides probiotics for gut health, while walnuts support brain and thyroid health with omega-3s.

Prep time: 5 minutes
Serving: 1

Ingredients:
- 1/2 cup full-fat coconut yogurt
- 1 tbsp chopped walnuts
- 1 tsp honey

Instructions:
1. Top coconut yogurt with walnuts and drizzle with honey.

Nutritional Info (Per Serving):
Calories: 180 kcal
Fats: 11 g (4 g saturated)
Carbohydrates: 12 g (2 g fiber, 8 g sugar)
Protein: 8 g

Key nutrients: Probiotics, Omega-3 Fatty Acids, Magnesium

8. Carrot Sticks with Red Pepper Hummus

Carrots are rich in vitamin A, which supports eye health and immune function. The olive oil and chickpeas in the hummus provide healthy fats and protein while being rich in antioxidants and fiber.

Prep time: 10 minutes (if using store-bought hummus)
Serving: 2

Ingredients:
- 4-5 large carrots, peeled and cut into sticks
- 1 cup of roasted red pepper hummus (store-bought or homemade)

For homemade hummus:
- 1 can (15 oz) of chickpeas, drained and rinsed
- 1 roasted red bell pepper
- 2 tbsp tahini

- 1 garlic clove
- 2 tbsp olive oil
- 1 tbsp lemon juice
- Salt and pepper to taste

Instructions:
1. If making homemade hummus, blend the chickpeas, roasted red pepper, tahini, garlic, olive oil, and lemon juice in a food processor until smooth. Season with salt and pepper.
2. Serve the hummus in a bowl with carrot sticks on the side for dipping.

Nutritional Info (Per Serving):
Calories: 150 kcal (per serving)
Fats: 8 g (1 g saturated)
Carbohydrates: 16 g (5 g fiber, 5 g sugar)
Protein: 4 g

Key nutrients: Beta-Carotene, Vitamin E, Folate

9. Celery Sticks with Almond Butter

Almond butter supplies magnesium and selenium, while celery provides a hydrating and crunchy base.

Prep time: 3 minutes
Serving: 1

Ingredients:
- 2 celery sticks, cut into halves
- 2 tbsp almond butter

Instructions:
1. Spread almond butter along the length of each celery stick.
2. Serve immediately for a crunchy and satisfying snack.

Nutritional Info (Per Serving):
Calories: 160 kcal
Fats: 13 g (1.5 g saturated)
Carbohydrates: 6 g (3 g fiber, 2 g sugar)
Protein: 4 g

Key nutrients: Magnesium, Vitamin K, Calcium

10. Thyroid-Friendly Energy Bites

These no-bake energy bites are packed with nutrients like omega-3s and healthy fats.

Prep time: 10 minutes (+30 minutes refrigeration)
Serving: 2 (2 bites per serving)

Ingredients:
- 1/2 cup almond flour
- 1/4 cup ground flaxseeds
- 2 tbsp coconut oil
- 1 tbsp honey
- 1/2 tsp cinnamon

Instructions:
1. Mix all ingredients in a bowl until a dough forms.
2. Roll into small balls and refrigerate for 30 minutes.

Nutritional Info (Per Serving):
Calories: 140 kcal (per serving)
Fats: 12 g (5 g saturated)
Carbohydrates: 7 g (2 g fiber, 3 g sugar)
Protein: 3 g

Key nutrients: Omega-3 Fatty Acids, Magnesium, Vitamin E

Chapter 9: Desserts

Indulging in desserts can be a truly joyful experience, and it doesn't have to come at the expense of your health—especially when you choose options that are naturally sweetened, gluten-free, and dairy-free. Dessert lovers rejoice! You can treat yourself while still nurturing your body and supporting your thyroid health. In this chapter, we dive into ten thoughtfully crafted dessert recipes that strike the perfect balance between delicious indulgence and wholesome nutrition. These creations are more than just desserts; they're a celebration of flavor, texture, and nourishment.

Each recipe has been designed with thyroid-friendly ingredients that prioritize your health without sacrificing taste. By avoiding refined sugars and dairy, these desserts focus on natural sweetness and nutrient-dense ingredients, offering a guilt-free way to satisfy your sweet tooth. Whether you're in the mood for a creamy mousse, a refreshing fruit-based delight, or a hearty baked treat, these recipes are simple to follow and packed with benefits for your body. Prepare to savor every bite as you explore how easy it is to enjoy desserts that are as good for your health as they are for your soul!

1. Almond Flour Chocolate Chip Cookies

Almond flour provides selenium and healthy fats, essential for thyroid hormone production and function.

Prep Time: 10 minutes
Cooking Time: 12 minutes
Servings: 12 cookies

Ingredients:
- 1 ½ cups almond flour
- ¼ cup coconut sugar
- 1 egg
- 1 tsp vanilla extract
- ¼ cup coconut oil, melted
- ½ tsp baking soda
- ¼ cup dark chocolate chips

Instructions:
1. Preheat your oven to 350°F (175°C) and line a baking sheet with parchment paper.
2. In a mixing bowl, whisk together the almond flour, coconut sugar, and baking soda until well combined.
3. In a separate small bowl, beat the egg, then add it to the dry ingredients. Pour in the melted coconut oil and vanilla extract. Mix everything together until a soft dough forms.
4. Fold in the dark chocolate chips until evenly distributed throughout the dough.
5. Scoop tablespoon-sized portions of dough onto the prepared baking sheet, spacing them about 2 inches apart. Flatten each cookie slightly with the back of a spoon.
6. Bake for 10-12 minutes or until the edges are golden brown.
7. Allow the cookies to cool on the baking sheet for a few minutes before transferring them to a wire rack to cool completely.

Nutritional Info (Per Cookie):
Calories: 130 kcal
Fats: 10g (2g saturated)
Carbohydrates: 8g (1g fiber, 5g sugar)
Protein: 3g

Key Nutrients: Selenium, vitamin E, magnesium

Tip: Store these cookies in an airtight container for up to a week to keep them fresh and chewy. For an extra twist, add a pinch of sea salt on top after baking.

2. Dairy-Free Coconut Ice Cream

Coconut milk offers medium-chain triglycerides (MCTs) that support energy production and metabolic function, vital for thyroid health.

Prep Time: 10 minutes
Cooking Time: 25 minutes (churning)
Servings: 6

Ingredients:
- 2 cans full-fat coconut milk
- ¼ cup maple syrup
- 1 tsp vanilla extract
- Pinch of sea salt

Instructions:
1. In a medium-sized mixing bowl, whisk together the coconut milk, maple syrup, vanilla extract, and sea salt until smooth and well-combined.
2. Pour the mixture into an ice cream maker and churn according to the manufacturer's instructions (usually around 20-25 minutes) until the mixture reaches a soft-serve consistency.
3. If you don't have an ice cream maker, pour the mixture into a shallow dish and place it in the freezer. Stir every 30 minutes for 2-3 hours to prevent ice crystals from forming.
4. Once the ice cream has thickened, transfer it to an airtight container and freeze for another hour or until firm.
5. Optional: Toast coconut flakes in a dry skillet over medium heat until golden and sprinkle over the ice cream before serving for a crunchy topping.

Nutritional Info (Per Serving):
Calories: 250 kcal
Fats: 22g (18g saturated)
Carbohydrates: 14g (1g fiber, 12g sugar)
Protein: 2g

Key Nutrients: Lauric acid, manganese

Tip: Add toasted coconut flakes or dark chocolate shavings as toppings for added texture and flavor.

3. Gluten-Free Apple Crisp Recipe

Apples contain antioxidants like quercetin, while the topping provides healthy fats and fiber to support metabolic balance.

Prep Time: 15 minutes
Cooking Time: 35 minutes
Servings: 6

Ingredients:
- 4 large apples, peeled and sliced
- ½ cup almond flour
- ¼ cup rolled oats (make sure they're certified gluten-free)
- ¼ cup maple syrup
- 1 tsp ground cinnamon (divided)
- 3 tbsp coconut oil, melted
- ¼ tsp sea salt

Instructions:

1. Preheat the oven to 350°F (175°C).
2. In a baking dish, toss the sliced apples with ½ tsp cinnamon to evenly coat them.
3. In a separate bowl, mix the almond flour, oats, remaining ½ tsp cinnamon, melted coconut oil, maple syrup, and sea salt until you get a crumbly topping.
4. Spread this topping evenly over the cinnamon-coated apples.
5. Bake in the preheated oven for 35-40 minutes, or until the topping turns golden brown and the apples are tender.
6. Serve warm and enjoy your gluten-free apple crisp!

Nutritional Info (Per Serving):
Calories: 180 kcal
Fats: 9g (4g saturated)
Carbohydrates: 29g (5g fiber, 14g sugar)
Protein: 3g

Key Nutrients: Fiber, quercetin, manganese

Tip: Serve warm with a dollop of coconut yogurt or a drizzle of maple syrup for extra indulgence.

4. Chocolate Avocado Mousse

Avocados supply healthy fats and potassium, while cocoa powder offers magnesium, both essential for thyroid function.

Prep Time: 5 minutes
Cooking Time: 30 minutes (chilling)
Servings: 4

Ingredients:
- 2 ripe avocados
- ¼ cup unsweetened cocoa powder
- ¼ cup maple syrup
- 1 tsp vanilla extract
- 2 tbsp almond milk
- Mint leaf and berries (for garnish)

Instructions:
1. In a blender or food processor, combine the avocados, cocoa powder, maple syrup, vanilla extract, and almond milk. Blend until smooth and creamy, scraping down the sides as needed to ensure everything is well incorporated.
2. Taste the mousse and adjust the sweetness by adding more maple syrup if desired.
3. Spoon the mousse into serving dishes and refrigerate for at least 30 minutes to chill and thicken.
4. Before serving, garnish with a fresh mint leaf and a few berries for a pop of color and added flavor.

Nutritional Info (Per Serving):
Calories: 220 kcal
Fats: 15g (2g saturated)
Carbohydrates: 22g (5g fiber, 12g sugar)
Protein: 3g

Key Nutrients: Potassium, magnesium, vitamin E

Tip: Chill the mousse in individual serving glasses for a more elegant presentation. Top with shredded dark chocolate for added richness.

5. Coconut Macaroons

Coconut supports energy metabolism with MCTs, while the egg whites add protein and selenium.

Prep Time: 10 minutes
Cooking Time: 18 minutes
Servings: 12 macaroons

Ingredients:
- 2 cups unsweetened shredded coconut
- ¼ cup coconut flour
- ¼ cup maple syrup
- 2 egg whites
- 1 tsp vanilla extract
- Pinch of salt

Instructions:
1. Preheat the oven to 350°F (175°C). Line a baking sheet with parchment paper.
2. Mix the dry ingredients: In a large bowl, combine the shredded coconut, coconut flour, maple syrup, vanilla extract, and a pinch of salt. Stir well to combine.
3. Whip the egg whites: In a separate bowl, whisk the egg whites until stiff peaks form. This helps the macaroons hold their shape and adds lightness.
4. Fold the egg whites into the coconut mixture gently, making sure not to deflate them.
5. Shape the macaroons: Scoop small spoonfuls of the mixture (about 1 tablespoon each) onto the prepared baking sheet, spacing them slightly apart.
6. Bake for 15-18 minutes, or until the tops are golden brown and the edges are crispy.
7. Cool the macaroons on the baking sheet for a few minutes before transferring them to a wire rack to cool completely.

Nutritional Info (Per Macaroon):
Calories: 90 kcal
Fats: 7g (5g saturated)
Carbohydrates: 7g (2g fiber, 5g sugar)
Protein: 2g

Key Nutrients: Selenium, lauric acid, fiber

Tip: For extra flavor, drizzle melted dark chocolate over the macaroons after they have cooled. Store in an airtight container to maintain crispness.

6. Baked Pears with Cinnamon and Walnuts

Walnuts provide omega-3 fatty acids, while pears are rich in antioxidants and fiber to support thyroid and digestive health.

Prep Time: 5 minutes
Cooking Time: 25 minutes
Servings: 6

Ingredients:
- 3 ripe pears, halved and cored
- 2 tbsp maple syrup
- ¼ cup chopped walnuts
- ½ tsp ground cinnamon
- 1 tbsp coconut oil, melted

Instructions:
1. Preheat the oven to 350°F (175°C).
2. Prepare the pears: Slice the pears in half and carefully remove the cores. Arrange the pear halves cut side up in a baking dish.
3. Drizzle and top: Pour the melted coconut oil and maple syrup over the pears. Sprinkle them with chopped walnuts and ground cinnamon.
4. Bake for 20-25 minutes, or until the pears are tender and slightly caramelized.
5. Serve warm, either on their own or with a dollop of yogurt or whipped cream if desired.

Nutritional Info (Per Serving):
Calories: 140 kcal
Fats: 7g (2g saturated)
Carbohydrates: 23g (4g fiber, 14g sugar)
Protein: 2g

Key Nutrients: Omega-3 fatty acids, fiber, manganese

Tip: Serve these pears warm with a drizzle of maple syrup for extra indulgence.

7. Cashew Date Energy Balls

Dates provide natural sweetness and potassium, while cashews offer zinc and magnesium, essential for thyroid function.

Prep Time: 10 minutes
Cooking Time: None (refrigeration: 30 minutes)
Servings: 12 balls

Ingredients:
- 1 cup cashews
- 1 cup pitted dates
- 2 tbsp coconut oil
- 1 tsp vanilla extract
- Pinch of sea salt

Instructions:
1. Grind the cashews: In a food processor, pulse the cashews until finely ground, but don't over-process them into butter.
2. Blend the mixture: Add the pitted dates, coconut oil, vanilla extract, and a pinch of sea salt to the ground cashews. Blend until the mixture forms a sticky dough.
3. Form the balls: Scoop out the dough and roll it into bite-sized balls using your hands. You should get about 12 energy balls.
4. Chill: Place the energy balls in the refrigerator for at least 30 minutes to firm up before serving.

Nutritional Info (Per Ball):
Calories: 110 kcal
Fats: 6g (1.5g saturated)
Carbohydrates: 14g (2g fiber, 11g sugar)
Protein: 2g

Key Nutrients: Zinc, magnesium, potassium

Tip: For added flavor, roll the balls in shredded coconut or cacao powder before chilling.

8. Banana Almond Nice Cream

This dairy-free ice cream is a blend of frozen bananas and almond butter for a creamy, guilt-free dessert rich in potassium, selenium and vitamin E.

Prep Time: 5 minutes
Cooking Time: None (optional freezing: 1-2 hours)
Servings: 4

Ingredients:
- 4 frozen bananas, sliced
- 2 tbsp almond butter
- 1 tsp vanilla extract

Instructions:
1. Blend the ingredients: In a high-speed blender, add the frozen banana slices, almond butter, and vanilla extract.
2. Blend until smooth: Blend until the mixture becomes smooth and creamy, similar to soft-serve ice cream.
3. Serve immediately for a soft-serve texture, or transfer to a container and freeze for 1-2 hours for a firmer consistency.
4. Optional garnish: Top with additional banana slices, a drizzle of almond butter, or a sprinkle of chopped almonds for extra flavor and texture.

Nutritional Info (Per Serving):
Calories: 150 kcal
Fats: 4g (1g saturated)
Carbohydrates: 32g (3g fiber, 16g sugar)
Protein: 2g

Key Nutrients: Potassium, selenium, vitamin E

Tip: Serve immediately for a soft-serve texture, or freeze longer for a firmer consistency. Garnish with chopped nuts for added crunch.

9. Frozen Yogurt Bark with Berries and Almonds

This yogurt is rich in probiotics, antioxidants, and healthy fats, providing a nutritious boost that supports gut health, immune function, and thyroid wellness.

Prep Time: 5 minutes
Cooking Time: None (freezing: 2-3 hours)
Servings: 8

Ingredients:
- 2 cups dairy-free coconut yogurt
- 2 tbsp maple syrup
- ½ cup mixed berries (blueberries, strawberries, raspberries)
- ¼ cup sliced almonds
- 1 tsp vanilla extract

Instructions:
1. Line a baking sheet with parchment paper.
2. In a bowl, mix the coconut yogurt, maple syrup, and vanilla extract.
3. Spread the yogurt mixture evenly onto the lined baking sheet.
4. Sprinkle the mixed berries and sliced almonds on top of the yogurt.
5. Freeze for 2-3 hours until firm.
6. Once frozen, break into pieces and enjoy. Store leftovers in the freezer.

Nutritional Info (Per Serving):
Calories: 110 kcal
Fats: 7g (6g saturated)
Carbohydrates: 10g (2g fiber, 7g sugar)
Protein: 3g

Key Nutrients: Probiotics, antioxidants, vitamin C

Tip: Store the bark in an airtight container in the freezer for up to two weeks for a quick snack.

10. No-Bake Chocolate Coconut Bars

These bars offer healthy fats, antioxidants, and fiber from ingredients like coconut oil and almond flour, making them a thyroid-friendly, energy-sustaining treat.

Prep Time: 10 minutes
Cooking Time: None (refrigeration: 60 minutes)
Servings: 8

Ingredients:
- 1 cup shredded unsweetened coconut
- ½ cup coconut oil, melted
- ¼ cup maple syrup
- ½ cup dark chocolate chips (dairy-free)
- 1 tsp vanilla extract

Instructions:
1. In a mixing bowl, combine shredded coconut, melted coconut oil, maple syrup, and vanilla extract. Stir until well combined.
2. Press the mixture into a parchment-lined baking dish and refrigerate for 30 minutes to set.
3. In a small saucepan, melt the dark chocolate chips over low heat.
4. Pour the melted chocolate over the coconut base, spreading it evenly.
5. Place back in the fridge for another 30 minutes until the chocolate is firm.
6. Cut into bars and enjoy. Store in the fridge for a quick, no-bake treat.

Nutritional Info (Per Serving):
Calories: 180 kcal
Fats: 16g (13g saturated)
Carbohydrates: 10g (2g fiber, 7g sugar)
Protein: 1g

Key Nutrients: Lauric acid, fiber, magnesium

Tip: Cut the bars into smaller bite-sized pieces for portion-controlled snacks, and store them in the fridge for freshness.

Conclusion: Your Journey to Wellness

As we come to the end of this culinary journey, it's worth taking a moment to celebrate. You've ventured through a world of flavors, ingredients, and recipes that not only support your thyroid health but also invite you to savor every bite along the way. This cookbook has been designed as more than just a collection of recipes—it's your guide to nourishing your body with intention, joy, and mindfulness.

When it comes to food, we often think about what we should avoid or restrict, but the goal here is different. It's about abundance—the abundance of nutrient-rich foods that help you thrive, the abundance of energy that comes from fueling your body well, and the abundance of satisfaction that comes from enjoying meals that are not only good for you but taste great too. You've now experienced firsthand how simple, accessible ingredients can transform into something vibrant, delicious, and profoundly nourishing.

While each recipe in this book is carefully crafted to support your thyroid and overall well-being, they also serve as an invitation. An invitation to experiment, to find joy in the process of cooking, and to make these dishes your own. Whether it's adding your favorite herbs, adjusting the flavors to suit your palate, or discovering new pairings, the kitchen is now your playground.

You've seen how a few mindful ingredients can create a snack that fuels your energy, a meal that brings warmth and comfort, or a dessert that feels indulgent without any guilt. But what's most important is how these meals make you feel—energized, balanced, and cared for.

Cooking for yourself or your loved ones is one of the simplest, most powerful acts of self-care. When you take the time to prepare a meal, you're doing more than just putting food on the table. You're nourishing your body, supporting your thyroid health, and showing yourself that you deserve to feel vibrant and strong. Every dish you prepare is a reminder that your well-being is worth the time and effort.

But self-care doesn't mean perfection. There will be days when you whip up a simple, no-cook snack, and other days when you experiment with a full, flavorful dinner. Both are acts of love. Both are valuable.

Now that you've explored these recipes, this is just the beginning of a lifelong journey. There's so much more to discover in the world of thyroid-friendly foods, and every meal is an opportunity to reconnect with your body and its needs. Take what you've learned, but don't be afraid to play. Swap out ingredients, try something new, or reinvent your favorite dishes in ways that make you excited to be in the kitchen.

Remember, food is meant to be enjoyed. It's a way to connect with yourself, your health, and even your loved ones. Sharing these recipes can create moments of joy and togetherness, bringing nourishment not just to your body but to your soul as well.

Lastly, celebrate how far you've come. It's easy to get caught up in the rush of daily life, but by taking this step toward better health, you've already made a significant shift. You've chosen to prioritize what your body needs, to listen to its signals, and to care for it in a holistic way. That's something worth honoring.

This cookbook may end here, but your journey with food is ongoing. Each day, you have the chance to make choices that support your vitality, lift your energy, and bring a sense of well-being into every corner of your life. You don't need to do it perfectly; you just need to keep doing it with intention and joy.

So, where do you go from here? The answer is anywhere you like. Let your curiosity guide you to new recipes, new flavors, and new ways to feel your best. You've already taken the first step by learning, experimenting, and exploring the power of nourishing, thyroid-friendly meals.

As you continue this journey, remember that the kitchen is a place where wellness meets creativity, and the choices you make here ripple out into your entire life. Here's to many more delicious, health-filled moments, and to the vibrant, thriving future that awaits.

With love, health, and a bit of fun in the kitchen—keep cooking, keep exploring, and most importantly, keep enjoying every bite.

Your body will thank you for it.